Issue 1 March 1999

Edited by Dr. Valerie Steele

Fashion Theory

The Journal of Dress, Body & Culture

BERG

Fashion Theory: The Journal of Dress, Body & Culture

Editor
Dr. Valerie Steele
The Museum at the Fashion Institute of Technology, E201
Seventh Avenue at 27th Street
New York, NY 10001-5992
USA
Fax: +1 212 924 3958
e-mail: steelemajor@earthlink.net

Aims and Scope
The importance of studying the body as a site for the deployment of discourses is well-established in a number of disciplines. By contrast, the study of fashion has, until recently, suffered from a lack of critical analysis. Increasingly, however, scholars have recognized the cultural significance of self-fashioning, including not only clothing but also such body alterations as tattooing and piercing. *Fashion Theory* takes as its starting point a definition of 'fashion' as the cultural construction of the embodied identity. It aims to provide an interdisciplinary forum for the rigorous analysis of cultural phenomena ranging from footbinding to fashion advertising.

Anyone wishing to submit an article, interview, or a book, film or exhibition review for possible publication in this journal should contact Valerie Steele (at the address listed below) or the Editorial Department at Berg (150 Cowley Road, Oxford, OX4 1JJ, UK; e-mail: enquiry@berg.demon.co.uk).

Notes for Contributors can be found at the back of the journal.

ISSN: 1362-704X

Ordering Information	Four issues per volume.	One volume per annum.	1999: Volume 3

By mail:	Berg Publishers, 150 Cowley Road, Oxford, OX4 1JJ, UK.		
By fax:	+44 (0) 1865 791165		
By telephone:	+44 (0) 1865 245104		
By e-mail:	enquiry@berg.demon.co.uk		

Inquiries	Editorial: Kathryn Earle, Managing Editor, e-mail: kearle@berg1.demon.co.uk		
	Production: Sara Everett, e-mail: severett@berg.demon.co.uk		
	Advertising + subscriptions: Jenny Hudson, e-mail: jhudson@berg.demon.co.uk		

Subscription Rates:	Institutional base list subscription price: £86.00, US$120.00.	Individuals' subscription price: £35.00, US$48.00.	

Reprints of Individual Articles	Copies of individual articles may be obtained from the Publishers at the appropriate fees. Write to: Berg, 150 Cowley Road, Oxford, OX4 1JJ, UK.	Printed in the United Kingdom. MARCH 1999	

Contents

Editor
Dr. Valerie Steele
The Museum at the Fashion
    Institute of Technology, E201
Seventh Avenue at 27th Street
New York, NY 10001-5992
USA

Fax +1 212 924 3958
e-mail: steelemajor@earthlink.net

BERG

Fashion Theory, Volume 3, Issue 1, pp.1–2
Reprints available directly from the Publishers.
Photocopying permitted by licence only.

© Roxanne Lowit

Letter from the Editor

"Fetishism . . . is based on the sex-appeal of the inorganic," wrote Walter Benjamin, who believed that fetishism lay at the heart of modern fashion. "In every fashion perversions are intended and worn in the most reckless manner. Every fashion is at war with the organic. Every fashion couples the living body to the inorganic world . . ." In this issue of *Fashion Theory*, Barbara Vinken extends Benjamin's analysis of fetishism as the magical oscillation between the animate and the inanimate which is staged in fashion: "the trophy of the dead animal on the living body, the mask of make-up on the living face, the precious gems that cover the body with minerals or, yet more radically, fashion's body as a doll's body set in motion."

Moving beyond the familiar idea that the femininity is a travesty or masquerade, Vinken suggests that transvestism, "the travesty of this travesty," is the secret of *haute couture*, which accordingly has a "hyperfetishistic structure" that "topples literal, unmarked masculinity" and represents "the impossibility of *not* wearing a mask." Fashion is cross-dressing—man into woman, woman into man—but also the transgression of class boundaries—woman into dandy. This is an idea that has long intrigued me. In my book, *Paris Fashion: A Cultural History* (OUP, 1985; revised edition, Berg, 1998), I explored the idea of the dandy as "the black prince of elegance." Similarly, I discussed the dandyism of Coco Chanel in my book *Women of Fashion* (Rizzoli, 1991), where I quoted Chanel's statement to Salvador Dali about changing men's clothes into women's. In her article, Vinken goes on to analyze the work of designers such as Jean Paul Gaultier and Martin Margiela, Vivienne Westwood and Rei Kawakubo, who present new types of masculinity and femininity.

The mask and the mirror are the starting point for Caroline Evan's brilliant analysis of the fashion designs of Elsa Schiaparelli. Like Vinken, Evans addresses the themes of masquerade and performativity, but she seeks to ground them historically in Schiaparelli's life and times. In particular, she analyzes certain key pieces of Schiaparelli's work from 1937-38, such as her Shoe Hat and Ensemble and her Tear-Illusion Evening Dress (both of which were designed in collaboration with Salvador Dali), as well as the decor of her shop, which Jean Cocteau famously described as "a devil's laboratory. Women who go there fall into a trap, and come out masked or disguised." Apparently "frivolous" (or "feminine"), Schiaparelli's designs could also be interpreted as deconstructing the idea of fixed identities, "in favor of the shifting and uncertain meanings of a subject in progress."

This issue of *Fashion Theory* also contains other theoretically sophisticated articles which interrogate the meaning(s) of cultural practices as diverse as female veiling in the Islamic world and contemporary female tattooing. Finally, as always, the journal contains book and exhibition reviews. In light of the number of interesting fashion books and exhibitions being produced today, I would like to encourage contributions in this area.

Sincerely yours,

Valerie Steele

Fashion Theory, Volume 3, Issue 1, pp.3–32
Reprints available directly from the Publishers.
Photocopying permitted by licence only.

Masks, Mirrors and Mannequins: Elsa Schiaparelli and the Decentered Subject

Caroline Evans

Caroline Evans is Senior
Lecturer in Cultural Studies at
Central Saint Martins College
of Art and Design, London

Preface

The mask and the mirror are the starting-point for this analysis of the
designs of Elsa Schiaparelli from approximately 1937 to 1939. Through
Schiaparelli's life and work, the *leitmotifs* of identity, masquerade and
performativity (Butler 1990) sound a persistent chord—in her so-called
Surrealist designs of 1936–39, in her salon and boutique decor and her
fashion shows of the same period, in her social and professional links
with, on the one hand, Parisian high society and, on the other, many of
the artists associated with the Surrealist movement. An examination of
her work and her personal circumstances in the broader context of the

1930s, particularly of the history of ideas and its relation to politics and society, reveals that, far from being an oddity or an exception, she in fact typifies many of the concerns of her age.

These concerns are examined here in relation to Joan Rivière's essay on masquerade (1929) (Burgin *et al.* 1986 35–44) and Jacques Lacan's lecture on the Mirror Stage (1936) (Lacan 1977: 1–7) and his later writing on masquerade. The circular logic connecting these themes is that of the cultural construction of gender, whose operations are nowhere more clearly elaborated in the field of representation than in Schiaparelli's fashion designs. Initially the masquerade and the mirror are used as critical stratagems to interpret the designs; but these metaphors are subsequently subjected to a different scrutiny, one that grounds them historically in Schiaparelli's life and times. Rather than simply using contemporary (fashionable) theories of identity to interpret fashion from the 1930s, this article seeks to locate changing models of the self historically, and to map the development of the modern "decentered subject" in the inter-war years. A plea for old-fashioned historical materialism, it attempts to reconcile the interpretative stratagems of contemporary critical theory with a materialist analysis, not only of the fashion designs in question but also of the theory itself.

The "decentered subject" is topical, and its current fashionability tells us a great deal about contemporary concerns, and suggests why we might be interested in Schiaparelli today. Could a 1990s model of identity serve to explain designs of the 1930s? Clearly not, or, rather, only at the expense of historical accuracy. Yet the contemporary fascination with the decentered subject should not blind us to the fact that its "decentering" has a history, even a pedigree. Since the nineteenth century the idea of the self as a sovereign, transcendent, unitary and knowing subject has gradually given way to the idea of a decentered self that is mired in, and constituted by, culture (Dean 1992: 1). The disenfranchisement of the self from nineteenth-century certainties was already manifest during Schiaparelli's working life, a period in which ideas about identity were changing as rapidly as they are today. A sense of the instability of the modern world in the period after the First World War grew in the 1920s and 1930s into a sense of modernity as shifting, insecure and rootless, a time without depth when meaning could be read off surfaces. As Mark M. Anderson has written of a slightly earlier period, "clothing functions here as a metaphor for the instability and contingency of modern life, which has migrated to the surface of things" (Anderson 1992: 13). It is against this backdrop that Schiaparelli's theatrical designs may be argued to be predicated on the notion of a subject in process.

Some of the intellectual history of this backdrop is explored in Carolyn Dean's *The Self and Its Pleasures: Bataille, Lacan and the History of the Decentered Subject*, a book that treats "ideas as historical practices" (1992: 3), and that explores the ways in which, in the 1920s and 1930s, the stability of identity was perceived as being under threat in many discourses, both conservative and progressive. These included those of art, philosophy, psychiatry, psychoanalysis, and criminology: the self was rethought in many different spheres of "knowledge" and Dean argues that "Bataille and Lacan's formulation of decentered subjectivity [was] part of a cultural crisis in inter-war France in which all the criteria defining what makes a self and what gives it legitimacy were perceived as having dissolved" (1992: 3). *The Self and Its Pleasures* contextualizes the decentered subject of Lacan and Bataille in the inter-war years and argues that newly formulated ideas of "the self" are to be seen in the context of a myriad of changing discourses about identity. Schiaparelli's designs are part of an artistic avant-garde that was broad enough to include the work of the Surrealists as well as the early writings of Jacques Lacan. These are the topics covered by this article; but it should be remembered that, although the avant-garde had a vested interest in the dissolution of the self, it did not have a monopoly on it. At the same time, other, conservative, discourses, such as criminology and psychiatry (which amounted to a social hygiene movement) also reformulated questions of identity, albeit from a very different ideological position. After the First World War many writers and social commentators tried to rescue the idea of the sovereign self, but in the process only added to its dissolution. Schiaparelli's avant-garde practice must also be situated, both socially and economically, in the field of fashion, particularly as it relates to inter-war debates and anxieties about the "New Woman," many of which were focused on the troubling question of female dress and appearance.

The Masquerade

"A mask is not primarily what it represents but what it transforms" (Lévi-Strauss 1982: 144).

An analysis of a few key pieces of Schiaparelli's work from 1937–38, a period in which she worked in close collaboration with various artists, brings into focus the idea of masquerade in relation to her work: firstly, her Shoe Hat and Ensemble (Figure 1), which she designed in collaboration with Salvador Dalí, who did the initial sketch for the hat. The hat consists of a high-heeled black velvet inverted "shoe" worn with the toe projecting above the face, rather like a peaked cap. There was a second version in which the sole of the shoe was made in the bright pink that Schiaparelli named "shocking" and made her own. Gala Dalí modeled it in the all-black version. The black suit has lip-shaped buttons and embroidered and appliquéd lips for pockets. When the wearer slips her hand in her pocket she puts it into somebody's mouth . . . but whose? The intimacy of the mouth is juxtaposed against the elegant carapace of the fitted jacket; inside and outside become confused as Schiaparelli plays with different levels of signification on the surface of the body by

displacing and repositioning its parts through recognizably Surrealist tactics.

Joan Rivière's paper, *Womanliness as a Masquerade*, published nine years earlier in the *International Journal of Psychoanalysis* in 1929, provides a psychoanalytic counterpart to Schiaparelli's playful attitude toward the body, for it articulates female identity as a matter of surface, or appearance, destabilizing the idea of an essential femininity: "Womanliness therefore could be assumed and worn as a mask . . . The reader may now ask how I define womanliness or where I draw the line between womanliness and the 'masquerade.' My suggestion is not, however, that there is any such difference; whether radical or superficial, they are the same thing" (Burgin *et al.* 1986: 38). In Rivière's metaphor "the mask" operates something like clothing: it may either conceal or transform what is beneath. But as the quotation goes on to make clear, there *is* no "beneath." In its cultural construction, female identity is all front: it is modeled, or fabricated, on the surface—nowhere more so than in and through fashion. In Judith Butler's words, "gender is the repeated stylization of the body . . . [it] is a fantasy instituted and inscribed on the surface of bodies" (Butler 1990: 33).

Almost all Schiaparelli's displacements between the inside and the outside of the body are elaborated on the surface. A pair of suede gloves has red veins painted on the back of the hand and light blue piping at the wrist. The red veins suggest the interior of the body, but the pale blue piping suggests the skin on the back of the hand: are we inside or outside the body? In another pair, Schiaparelli appliqués red snakeskin nails onto black suede gloves: black suede or African skin? A grey linen jacket of 1937 with embroidery based on a drawing by the artist Jean Cocteau shows the silhouette of a woman at the shoulder, with embroidered and beaded golden "hair" tumbling down the right arm of the jacket. At the waist are embroidered the braceleted arm and hand of this fictional woman, clutching a pair of beaded gloves exactly where the real wearer might clasp her gloves, at waist level.

Schiaparelli's use of *trompe l'oeil* reveals women's bodies as a surface on which to play. In many of her garments there is no end to this play of surfaces, no "truth" beneath the "lie" of appearances. Masquerade does not imply that femininity is a lie so much as question its essential "truth." In the Judeo-Christian tradition there is a long history of women's being seen as duplicitous (Tseëlon 1995: 34–7). But in Schiaparelli's hands the theme of femininity as a form of choreographed deception (an old stand-by of misogynist myth and theology) becomes self-conscious, constructive and critical. "Tree bark" and "glass" fabrics, handbags resembling birdcages or telephones, buttons in the shape of peanuts, padlocks or typewriter keys, a "brain" hat of pink, corrugated velvet, a black "skeleton" dinner dress with embroidered ribs and spinal column: with these, and many other, feints she destabilizes the relation between reality and illusion and articulates femininity as being primarily

Figure 1
Elsa Schiaparelli, 1937. Black hat in the form of an inverted high-heeled shoe, designed in collaboration with Salvador Dali, worn with a black cocktail suit with pocket edges appliquéd in the shape of lips. Collection of The Costume Institute, The Metropolitan Museum of Art, New York. Photograph courtesy of The Fashion Institute of Technology, New York.

a matter of representation: "In the masquerade the woman mimics an authentic—genuine—womanliness, but then authentic womanliness is such a mimicry, *is* the masquerade ('they are the same thing') . . . the masquerade is a representation of femininity but then femininity is representation, the representation of the woman" (Stephen Heath in Burgin *et al.* 1986: 49, 53). Furthermore, this representation may be disconcerting rather than reassuring. A dress of 1938 is worn with matching black gloves with gold claws in place of fingernails. The golden talons bring an animal otherness to bear on the otherwise elegant and sumptuous evening dress, combining beauty with menace, desire with dread. Often her use of fur or insects likewise disturbs conventional associations with softness and femininity, as when she uses plastic cicada buttons on a jacket (1938) or sets colored insects in a clear plastic necklace to give the impression that they are crawling round the wearer's neck (c. 1937–8). Even more disconcertingly, the fur cuff on a pair of Perugia high-heeled suede ankle boots has been replaced by a long fringe of trailing monkey fur that bears a disturbing resemblance to human hair.

Masquerade and performativity together constitute a backdrop—the paradox of women's identity as non-identity, of surface as depth—against which Schiaparelli the fashion designer stages her performances. Women's bodies are the canvases upon which she paints her images of self-display. A contemporary press headline declared "Schiaparelli collection enough to cause crisis in vocabulary" (Schiaparelli 1954: 72). That crisis goes to the heart of "the self." If fashion is the glue that binds identity, in Schiaparelli's hands it becomes a solvent: through trickery, allusion and wit different layers of meaning are elaborated in a series of designs that, far from constructing identity as fixed, actually deconstructs it as a "becoming." In the process it destabilizes notions of the sovereign self, or the "subject," in favor of the shifting and uncertain meanings of a subject in process.

The Decentered Subject

Schiaparelli's designs from the late 1930s, and the concept of masquerade, could both be associated with the "decentered subject" developed in the writing of Lacan in the inter-war years (Dean 1992: 2). Dean argues that the "replotting" of the self is bound up with a series of historically and geographically located practices, rather than a broader shift in the paradigms of subjectivity (1992: 9). One such practice was the masquerade, which was closely linked to the rapidly changing lives of many modern women; contemporary fears about the New Woman were provoked by new representations and practices of femininity that challenged established certainties about women's social place. Joan Rivière's text of 1929 contributes, from a specifically female point of view, to a psychoanalytic discourse that reconfigures female identity as a result of social change—the incursion of women into the male world of the professions. Rivière, herself a professional woman, describes the behavior of a career woman at a speaking engagement who put on a masquerade of "womanliness"—flirting with her male audience—to fend off the charge of masculinity (Burgin *et al.* 1986: 37–8).

Psychoanalytically, Rivière relates masquerade to feminine lack, and in Lacan's account too (Lacan 1977: 289–90) women masquerade *as* the phallus (the signifier of desire) because they do not *have* it. "For Lacan, masquerade is the very definition of 'femininity' precisely because it is constructed with reference to a male sign" (Mitchell and Rose 1982: 43). Some of Lacan's references to the masquerade simply stereotype women as creatures who turn themselves, by way of self-adornment, into signifiers of desire, showing a "feminine" fondness for masks and masquerade ("scattered sociological observations being passed off as a theory of sexual difference," according to Bowie 1991: 143). But other references to the masquerade and melancholy are particularly à propos to develop the idea of alienation in relation to Schiaparelli. It is primarily Lacan, the theorist of alienation (as opposed to the theorist of sexual difference), who is relevant to this analysis. His account of identity in particular presents a self that is not whole and coherent but split and alienated.

Lacan, who lived and worked in Paris at the same time as Schiaparelli, began his clinical training in 1927, the year of her first design success, a *trompe-l'oeil* knitted jumper. Although their careers, interests and social worlds had nothing in common, both associated with the Surrealists in the 1930s, and particularly with Salvador Dalí, Schiaparelli's collaborator on the Shoe Hat and Tear-Illusion dress, as well as on other projects from the late 1930s. In the early 1930s Lacan shared an interest in paranoia with Dalí (who mentions him in a memoir); Lacan's doctoral dissertation of 1932 was on paranoia, and Bowie suggests that they influenced each other at this time (Bowie 1991: 39). He also suggests that Lacan's concept of "the body in bits and pieces" owes something to Hans Bellmer's *Doll* photographs, which appeared in the Surrealist journal *Minotaure* in 1936 (1991: 215). In 1933 Lacan published two articles in *Minotaure*, and a sonnet in *Le Phare de Neuilly*. His concept of the Mirror Stage was first formulated in 1936, the period of Schiaparelli's so-called Surrealist designs.[1] Interestingly, Malcolm Bowie has described Lacan's intellectual style in terms very similar to Schiaparelli's design stratagems. Bowie argues that, in all his writing, Lacan took issue with the dryness of the language of psychoanalyis and, instead, eroticized theory, so that the theoretical text could become "a moving simulacrum of desire in movement—a carnival, a masked ball . . . Lacan's writing seeks to tease and seduce. It is full of feints, subterfuges, evasions and mimicries. It unveils and re-veils its meanings from paragraph to paragraph." (1991: 200).

The anarchic and playful elements of the masked ball and carnival are caught in Schiaparelli's Circus collection of early 1938. Pale blue ponies prance over the pink silk twill evening jacket of Figure 2, which is fastened by painted metal flying trapeze-artist buttons. Another cocktail suit with clown-hat buttons was worn with a tall and pointed pink sequinned clown's hat. There were lavishly beaded boleros embroidered with circus elephants, spot-lit acrobats, tents and clowns, for which Lesage revived eighteenth- and nineteenth-century military embroidery techniques. The collection also featured the backwards suit, with lapels, buttons, cravat and brooch all on the back. There was a hat that was a nest with a hen sitting on it; crushed clown top-hats, some with insect brooches; and tall colored feathers like circus ponies', tied on with ribbons. Shoes were in gold crêpe rubber, and the first platform shoes were worn.

The Circus Collection, one of the first themed shows in Parisian *couture*, brings high fashion into a creative tension with the idea of fashioning the self as a coherent performance. The circus is a locus of spectacle, fun and abandon, but also a twilight world of refuge, danger and loss of self. Its feints and subterfuges establish it as an eroticized place, "a moving simulacrum of desire in movement" (Bowie 1991: 200): the theatrical space of instability. In similar vein, the Tear-Illusion Dress of 1937 (Figure 3) flirts with the darker side of fashion. Another Dalí/Schiaparelli collaboration, this elegant evening gown in silk crêpe is printed with a *trompe l'oeil* pattern of rips; it is worn with a headscarf in which the "rips" consist of appliquéd voile and silk flaps. The pale flesh-colored voile "rips" reveal darker purplish-pink silk beneath. They are the colors of bruised and torn flesh; yet it is completely unclear whether the illusion is meant to suggest torn fabric or flesh. Is the cloth below the "tears" textile or skin? Do the rips designate poverty (rags not riches) or some form of attack? Schiaparelli here plays with ideas normally antithetical to fashion, countering poise and tranquillity with violence and anxiety.

The somber note struck by the Tear-Illusion dress sounds again in the melancholic *Commedia dell'arte* collection of late 1938. This collection, featuring black tricorn hats worn with masks, makes the masquerade theme explicit (a Blumenfeld photograph shows one of the model's blond curls cut off and pinned to her hat). The *Commedia* theme is about love, but a tragic love: its characters are variously cuckolds or misfits. The audience is distanced from them, but they suffer and are alienated on our behalf. Schiaparelli's *coup de théâtre* is to make the wearer one of them, and in so doing to suggest that life is a masquerade, rather than a costume ball.

The connection between masquerade and melancholy is implicit in Lacan's account of the sexual comedy,[2] which frequently uses the metaphors of the mask and the veil to speak of the impossibility of the satisfaction of desire. The Lacanian subject is an alienated one, "haunted

Figure 2
Elsa Schiaparelli, 1938. Pink silk twill evening jacket adorned with circus ponies in pale blue and fastened with painted metal trapeze-artist buttons. From the collection of the Victoria and Albert Museum. Photograph courtesy of the Victoria and Albert Museum, London.

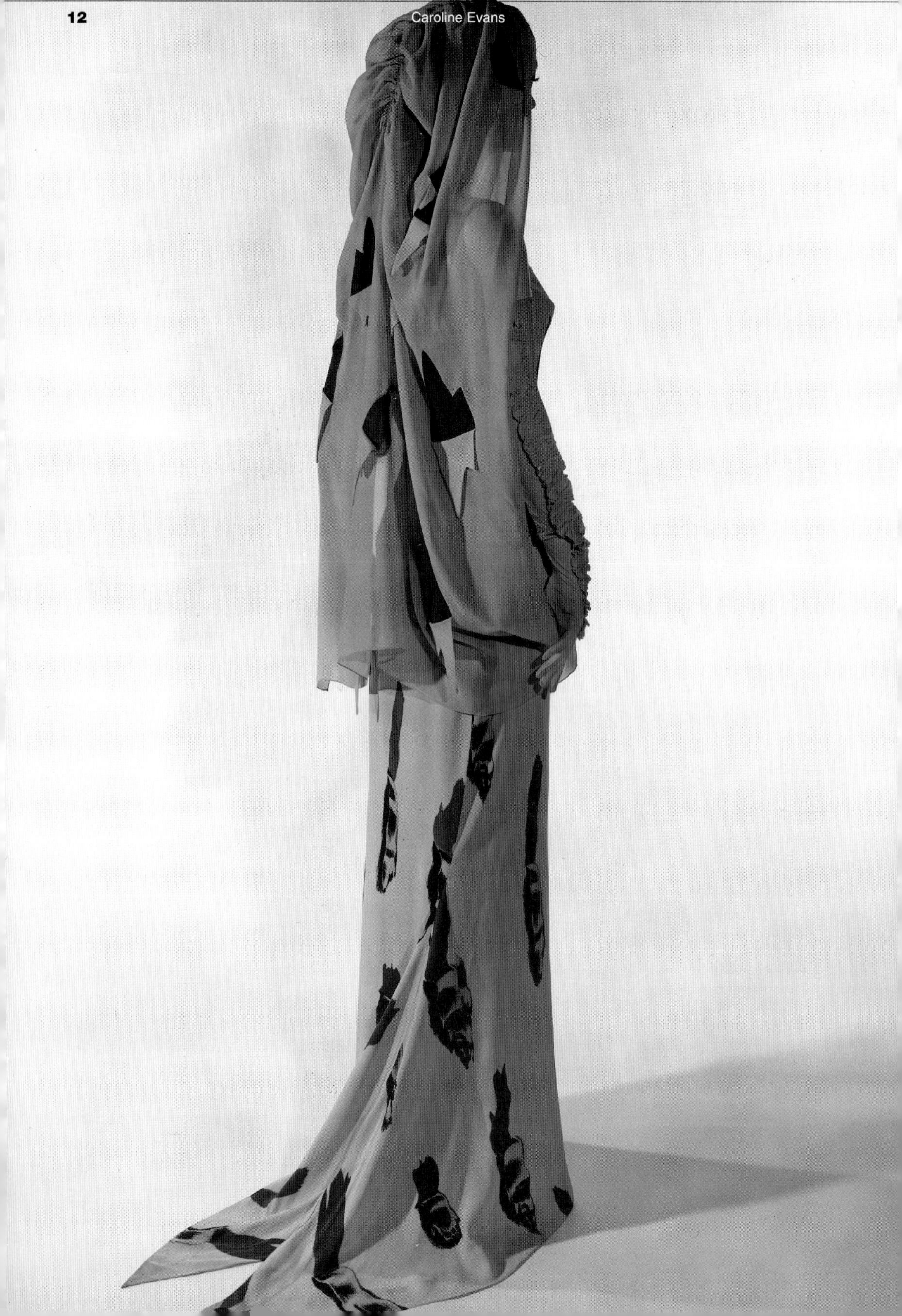

by absence and lack" (Bowie 1991: 135) and the expression of this melancholy state of affairs is the mask, whose function "dominates the identifications through which refusals of love are resolved" (Lacan 1977: 291). Judith Butler argues that the mask becomes

> part of the incorporative strategy of melancholy . . . The mask thus conceals this loss, but preserves (and negates) this loss through its concealment. The mask has a double function which is the double function of melancholy. The mask is taken on through the process of incorporation which is a way of inscribing and then wearing a melancholic identification in and on the body; in effect it is the signification of the body in the mold of the Other who has been refused (Butler 1990: 48, 49–50).

Indeed, Butler goes so far as to suggest that melancholic incorporation (in psychoanalysis, the internalization of a lost object of love—and the first lost object is the mother) may be not *in* the body but "*on* the body as its surface signification such that the body must itself be understood as an incorporated space" (1990: 67). In this light not only the *Commedia* collection, but also the Tear-Illusion Dress, or the Cocteau-inspired embroidered suit, can be rethought as examples of melancholy tracery, no longer playful and light-hearted but inscribed with the darker meanings of the decentered or split subject: alienation and loss, writ large on the body.

Although the feminist appropriation of the concept of masquerade provides a model of female agency within fashion ("woman can play the woman or not as she so pleases" (Wright 1992: 243)), this has been at the cost of some misreading of the original sources. Rivière's analysand found herself painfully caught in the role of masquerade, a defensive stratagem in a male world that did not always welcome women as equals, and Judith Butler reminds us of the regulatory role of the performative aspects of gender: "Performativity has to do with repetition, very often repetition of oppressive and painful gender norms to force them to resignify. This is not freedom, but a question of how to work the trap that one is inevitably in" (Kotz 1992: 83). We cannot pick and mix identities, only outfits. But some outfits can make explicit, even pleasurable, the working mechanism of the masquerade, with its potential for both comedy and tragedy. Perhaps in Schiaparelli's work we can discern something melancholic and alienated about fashion itself, particularly when it is at its most playful and extreme. But since fashion acts also as an interface between subjectivity and social meaning, it is perhaps hardly surprising that Schiaparelli's last themed collection in 1938, before the outbreak of the Second World War became inevitable, the *Commedia dell'arte* collection, was her most melancholic yet.

Figure 3
Elsa Schiaparelli, 1937. Tear-Illusion evening dress in silk crêpe printed with a pattern of rips designed by Salvador Dalí. It is worn with a shawl in which the rips are appliquéd flaps of fabric. From the collection in the Victoria and Albert Museum, London. Photograph courtesy of the Victoria and Albert Museum, London.

The Mirror

"I merely know Schiap by hearsay. I have only seen her in a mirror" (Schiaparelli 1954: ix).

With these words Elsa Schiaparelli opens her autobiography *Shocking Life*, a text that moves arbitrarily between first- and third-person narrative, in which, more often than not, she refers to herself in the third person as "Schiap." She goes on, still in the third person, to sketch her own character, which is full of interesting and impossible contradictions, and finally repeats, but with a new emphasis: "I have seen her in the mirror" (1954: ix). Later in her autobiography, however, she describes a scene of mis-recognition in the mirror, a night out in Berlin in the 1930s: "As I mounted the imposing staircase, surrounded by mirrors, I saw in the centre of a crowd of rather shabby people one who reminded me of Paris. 'There,' I said to Jerome, 'at last there is a smart woman!' 'Heavens!' exclaimed Jerome, 'but don't you recognize yourself?'" (1954: 107). The photographer Horst B. Horst's portrait photograph of her in 1937 shows an elegant woman in a dramatic, asymmetrical dark hat and gold-embroidered fitted jacket. Her image is contained in an oval frame which is commonly perceived as a mirror frame. Closer scrutiny reveals, however, that the "mirror" is in fact a hole in the wall, from which Schiaparelli's right forearm and left hand protrude slightly, to rest on the lower edge of the gilt *oeil-de-boeuf* frame. The effect is disconcerting, as if a two-dimensional image had suddenly come to life and leaned out of its frame. Horst plays on the ambiguity of the mirror and the picture frame, just as Lacan turns a mirror into a spectacle when he puns on the words "specular" and "spectacular," or turns mirror *images* into *mirages* (Bowie 1991: 36) by merging the words *miroir* and *image* to produce *mirage*. The picture shows us the "real" Schiaparelli, but we understand it to be an illusion—a mirror image. This slippage captures the slippery and illusory nature of the mirror—and of representation itself—that lies at the heart of Schiaparelli's work. Arguably, it lies at the heart of all fashion; but the mechanism is revealed in Schiaparelli's work. Whereas in, say, Vionnet's designs the masquerade of femininity is seamless, Schiaparelli tears the veil, pulls the masquerade away, and shows its workings by manipulating surface signifiers that she layers, or plays with, on the body.

Figure 4 shows a black velvet jacket with buttons of sculpted female heads, embroidered with upside-down hand mirrors by Lesage. Here Schiaparelli's decorative use of real mirrored glass operates in a complex and ambiguous way. The duplicated symbols of feminine vanity, two hand mirrors, are worn upside-down on the breast like armor. Like a Rococo anachronism, these mirrors evoke a fairy-tale hall of mirrors; thus upholstered clothes become like furniture, the body a stage set. It is the observer, not the wearer, whose fractured image is reflected back in the broken mirrors. If, as John Berger says, women are condemned to watch themselves being looked at, Schiaparelli pursues that problem into the theatre, throws up a cloud of spangles and, in the form of the splintered hand mirrors, turns the shattered gaze back on the spectator. The theatricality of all Schiaparelli's work shows an understanding of fashion as performance, or masquerade; the wearer creates herself as spectacle, but the moment she displays herself she also disguises herself: "the masquerade, in flaunting femininity, holds it at a distance" (Doane 1982: 81). By putting a distance between herself and her observers she makes a space within which to maneuver and to determine the meanings of the show (Evans and Thornton 1989: 141). Those meanings, however, are not fixed, but circular and ambiguous, for we encounter only a series of signs that refer us back to the surface—treacherous, slippery . . . a hall of mirrors from which there is no exit.

Figure 5 shows a self-portrait from 1928 by the French artist Claude Cahun, one of several taken over the previous eleven years in which the artist repeatedly refashioned her own image, staging herself in different settings and guises as, variously, male, female, or doll-like. From 1919 Cahun consciously rejected conventional femininity by shaving her head and sometimes dyeing the resulting stubble green or pink. Although ostensibly having nothing in common with fashion, in fact her work has much in common with Schiaparelli's. Both women were outsiders in their respective fields of art and design: Cahun was a Jew, an intellectual, and a lesbian; Schiaparelli an Italian divorcée who couldn't sew. David Bate's analysis of Cahun's photographic series could equally well apply to Schiaparelli's fashion designs, for the work of both shows "the cultural *coding* of the body rather than the body itself; costumes, masks, theatrical make-up and facial expression take precedence when compared with those other Surrealists' emphasis on the female body as *torso*" (Bate 1994: 8). In this image Cahun has staged herself with props that Schiaparelli uses in her collections of the late 1930s, the harlequin coat and the mirror. As in Figure 4, and as in the Horst portrait of Schiaparelli in the "mirror," so here Cahun disrupts the pictorial convention of narcissistic identification in which women are portrayed gazing at themselves in the mirror; instead she gazes out of the frame, thus producing a double, not a reflection; an other, not a self.

The convention of the unitary self is here disrupted in favor of the uncanny double; the mirror, far from confirming women's essential narcissism, deflects any dialogue between mirror and self in which the mirror acts as guarantor of identity. Rather, it produces the possibility of an alienated image, like the alienated self of Lacan's Mirror Stage, in which the ego is formed through a process of identification with the mirror image. From 6 to 18 months the infant begins to recognize and identify with its image in the mirror, or to see itself mirrored in the imitative behavior of another adult or child, and to derive from this an imaginary sense of wholeness. Thus the infant's sense of self is not innate,

Figure 4
Elsa Schiaparelli, 1939. Detail of a black velvet evening jacket showing Lesage embroidery of upside-down hand mirrors appliquéd with gold tinsel and pieces of real mirrored glass. The buttons are sculpted female heads. The jacket is worn with a long black dinner dress and a black plumed cap. From the collection of The Costume Institute, The Metropolitan Museum of Art, New York. Photograph courtesy of The Costume Institute, The Metropolitan Museum of Art, New York.

but constructed; and this construction is founded upon an illusion, for the unified image in the mirror is at odds with the actual helplessness of the infant. Our first recognition of ourselves is a mis-recognition, a fiction and a fantasy (Mitchell and Rose 1982: 30), a *mirage*, not an *image*. Furthermore, "the identification with its own body as an other constitutes the subject as his own rival, so that its very unity is permeated with distress, fragmentation, and aggressiveness" (Dean 1992: 50). Likewise, Schiaparelli's *mis*-recognition of her self in the Berlin night-club's mirror grants her an alienated image of herself as other; the same slippage between self and other occurs in the Horst portrait, and in

Figure 5
Claude Cahun, 1928. Self-portrait in a mirror. Photograph courtesy of Jersey Museums Service.

Cahun's self-portrait. Carolyn Dean argues that in this period psychiatrists, psychoanalysts and Surrealists all, in various ways, theorized and constructed the self out of a new, changing interest in the other, and, in doing so, unraveled it. Thus, she argues, self-dissolution is implicit in the construction of some forms of modern (and now postmodern) subjectivity (Dean 1992: 248–9, 251).

Even the phrase "Mirror Stage" is a pun: *Stade du Miroir* can also mean "stadium" of the mirror, a stadium in which the battle of the human subject is instigated at "the threshold of the visible world" (Lacan 1977: 3). Lacan's Mirror Stage makes explicit the alienation and misapprehension upon which identity is founded, while simultaneously proposing that modern identity is rooted in the visual—the image of the self as other. And just as in Lacan's theory this need not be an actual mirror, but may be behavior that reflects back a self-image, so in Schiaparelli's designs it may be the fashioned image that reflects back a sense of self. But the deconstructive power of the Mirror Suit is that it shatters the illusion, or fantasy, of wholeness, revealing that, in Susan Sontag's words, "the self is a text . . . a project, something to be built" (Benjamin 1992: 14).

The purpose of this discussion of Lacan's Mirror Stage is, firstly, to introduce the notion of an alienated or decentered subject, and relate it to fashion; secondly, to locate these ideas in the 1930s, a period in which the idea of the sovereign self came under attack from fashion and psychoanalysis equally; thirdly, to argue that in periods of rapid social change meaning mutates to the surface of things, and representation itself becomes a stadium in which competing definitions (here in relation to images of women) slug it out. The scopic regime of the mirror becomes the place in which the script of the self is written.

In her book *Showgirls* Andrea Stuart describes the showgirl at the beginning of the twentieth century as the epitome of the modern woman who performs herself into being. Far from being the passive object of the male gaze, the showgirl manufactures her own image: the mirror, in which she puts on her stage make-up, is "a tool of self-realization, a space where a woman becomes spectacle to herself, where she discovers and reinvents herself, where she quite literally makes herself up" (Stuart 1996: 71–2). In a fashion drawing for *Harper's Bazaar* of 1938 the illustrator Marcel Vertès shows us a Schiaparelli Inkpot Hat of glazed straw, with a large feather quill sticking up from it. He has drawn the wearer with her right hand raised to grasp the quill, as if she is just dipping it into the pot (the hat) prior to writing on the paper (signed "Vertès") in front of her. Here, perhaps, is Schiaparelli writing herself into existence or, perhaps, for she is a designer, drawing herself. Vertès' conceit is prescient: Schiaparelli, herself a self-made woman, contributed in no small degree to other women's self-definition in her fashion designs of the inter-war years.

The New Woman

> It has become very difficult to differentiate at first sight an honest woman or a pure young girl from a whore . . . All women, from the adolescent to the grandmother are molded according to the same model: they wear lipstick and powder their faces, have pearly eyelids, long black lashes, painted nails, platinum or red hair . . .; they all smoke, drink cocktails, loiter at dancing halls, drive cars . . . how can we place them? Which is the marquise, the wife of the wealthy industrialist? Or simply the woman of easy virtue? What an embarrassing question and what a difficult problem to solve (Dean 1992: 70).

Thus did a French commentator in 1934 articulate the "problem" of the New Woman, a "problem" that was seen to be as much one of appearances as of behavior. Women were given the vote in France only in 1945. The "New Woman," in the form of the sexually independent woman in particular, was a source of much anxiety in the inter-war years as she destabilized the conventional association between appearance and identity. In particular, it was important to social commentators to distinguish between prostitutes and respectable women, and this became progressively harder as make-up and fashion became universal, accessible to any woman who could afford them. "Masked with lipstick and rouge, all women were equally suspect" (Monahan 1995: 130). Whereas before the First World War a respectable woman would lightly powder her nose and cheeks, at the most adding a little rouge, throughout the 1920s a range of new preparations came on the market: nail varnish, false eyelashes, mascara and lipstick, which was even worn in the daytime (Cronin 1994: 47). The year 1927 saw the introduction of the first French lipstick, which, it was claimed, did not come off when kissing: *rouge à lèvres baiser*. Beauty parlors (*salons de beauté*) opened "where experts could help a lady to create her own facial beauty, not unlike a sculptor or a painter creating a work of art" (1994: 47). One of these was opened by the writer Colette in 1932, where she was photographed making up her adult daughter (Augé 1996: 170–1). The increasing popularity of dieting testified to a desire to modify the body internally as well as externally. Short hair, in the form of the Eton Crop (1927) and then the Marcel wave of the early 1930s, had compelled women to use the hairdresser more rather than less (Zeldin 1973 Vol. 2: 442). By the late 1930s regular and expensive visits to the hairdresser were part of most affluent women's beauty routine. But although a high degree of artifice was by now incorporated into women's self-image, it was never acknowledged to be artifice in the discourse of fashion. By contrast, Schiaparelli's introduction in 1939 of purple lipstick (called "frolic"), and in 1931 of silver, ash blond and red wigs (color coordinated to match evening dresses) destabilized the conventional association of women with nature and highlighted the artifice of the construction of femininity.

In addition, ideas about the unitary self were being destabilized from different quarters of intellectual life; in this climate it was easy for conservative commentators to seize on women's fashions as the work of the devil. Carolyn Dean comments on how the New Woman or *la garçonne* (the bachelor-girl) became "the symbolic centre of moral crisis" in this period (Dean 1992: 63). The New Woman's choice of her own sexual partners was taken by conservative critics to be a mark not of deviance but—worse—of masculinity, that awful capacity for gender fluidity that characterized the modern woman who usurped male prerogatives (1992: 71). Thus the "crisis" of male power was related to the fluidity of gender and, specifically, the mobility of femininity in its cultural construction—in make-up, masquerading fashions, and financial and sexual independence.

Schiaparelli herself was just such a New Woman. Not only does every photograph show her fashionably made-up and coiffed, but also the circumstances of her life define her as one of the new generation of independent women. She was a single parent, a working mother, a woman who, after her husband abandoned her and their small child, declined the emotional and financial support of her family and opted instead for independence. At this period she was not an established designer, and had no obvious means of supporting herself and her child. Financial circumstances and convention were against her doing what she did. Furthermore, she made a decision not to remarry, but to have, in the style of the New Woman, "a series of friendships, sometimes tender, sometimes detached, witty and sharp and short, full always of the same anxiety for privacy and freedom, battling incessantly for small liberties" (Schiaparelli 1954: 45).

Once she was established she remained the sole owner of her business, which was unusual in *haute couture* (White 1986: 85). It is also significant that Schiaparelli was an Italian in Paris couture, a business whose identity in the 1930s was, both financially and ideologically, emphatically French; she was therefore an outsider with perhaps the heightened awareness of issues connected to identity that outsiders have. Italians were often despised in this period in the world of fashion, as they had a reputation for fraudulently copying French designs. This fact gives a slightly different emphasis to Chanel's contemptuous reference to Schiaparelli as "that Italian who makes dresses" (Éditions Paris-Musées 1987: 26). Schiaparelli took French nationality, but, despite her adherence to France and the French, her Italian origins guaranteed that she always remained somewhat of an outsider in her adopted country, despite the fact that, as her autobiography makes clear, she had no sympathy with Italian Fascism in the 1930s. During the occupation of France she voluntarily returned from the USA to live in Paris; this was seen by the occupying Germans as a rejection of her Italian identity and a subversive identification with the occupied French. For this reason it became too dangerous for her to stay in Paris, and she was obliged to leave again, whereas had she been born a French citizen her presence there would have been less noteworthy, and she would have been able to remain and work throughout the war.

Outsider status confers a consciousness of identity as something culturally constructed. *Shocking Life* refers to an early desire for transformation: the six-year old Elsa, convinced she is ugly and wishing to become beautiful, plants flower seeds in her throat, mouth and ears in the hope that they will grow into a garden (Schiaparelli 1954: 7). The story may be apocryphal, but is entirely in keeping with Schiaparelli's emphasis on transformation and metamorphosis. Her status as a New Woman and as an outsider in France (and in fashion) may both have contributed to her use of masquerade, play and illusion in her designs. Palmer White says that women's clothes in 1930s had to conceal "the inner female." Although the theory of masquerade is a deconstructive one that runs counter to the very idea of an "inner female," nevertheless Palmer White's observations are not unlike Joan Rivière's. She argued in 1929 that professional women's masquerade was a reaction formation against the charge of "masculinization." Palmer White argues that women's clothes in the 1930s "had to protect the New Woman from counter-attacks by the male, whose superiority and domination she was challenging and whose territory she was invading" (White 1986: 96). Despite the apparent "frivolity" (coded "feminine") of her work, Schiaparelli invaded this territory both in her person and in her designs, and it is this particular set of historical circumstances that facilitated such a playful and deconstructive approach to dress at the heart of the quite conventional business of Paris couture, a deconstructive approach that is witty but also deadly serious.

The Devil's Laboratory

"Her establishment on the Place Vendôme is a devil's laboratory. Women who go there fall into a trap, and come out masked or disguised . . ." (White 1986: 179).

Thus did Jean Cocteau describe Schiaparelli's premises in 1937. The performative aspects of the masquerade, and the illusory effects of the mirror, were extended to Schiaparelli's presentation of her shop, her business and her shows. Whereas the previous sections looked at Schiaparelli's fashion designs and personal circumstances in relation to masquerade, the mirror and the decentered subject, this and the following section are devoted to the other areas of her designs: shop interiors, shows and exhibitions, and to her affiliations with the Surrealists, with whom she shared a deconstructive approach to reality.

In January 1935 the business moved to a Mansard building at 21 Place Vendôme; on the ground floor was the boutique, designed by Jean-Michel Franck. One part was in the form of a gilded bamboo cage for the perfume department. Giacometti made gold-leaf columns and shells for lamps. Bettina Jones (subsequently Bergery), an American model turned assistant to Schiaparelli, dressed the windows whose *outré* displays could be seen by passers-by *en route* to the nearby Ritz. These often included life-size mannequins or the stuffed bear that Dalí had dyed "shocking" pink and fitted with drawers in its stomach. Bettina Bergery dressed it in an orchid satin gown and loaded the drawers with jewels. Sometimes it sat in the salon on Dalí's lips sofa, based on the lips of Mae West, the ultimate spectacle-woman, which was upholstered in "shocking" pink fabric. This *boutique fantasque*, a commercial innovation since copied by other couturiers, became one of the sights of Paris. "Pascal was added to the staff. Pascal, of pure Greek beauty with golden hair, supple and dignified . . . continued to look with calm indifference at the gaping crowds" (Schiaparelli 1954: 71). Pascal was a wooden articulated mannequin chosen by Schiaparelli as a lucky mascot for the salon and boutique of Place Vendôme. Tall and glamorous, he is described by Schiaparelli as if he is a real person, thus further destabilizing the boundaries of identity, between human and dummy, animate and inanimate. Pascal often sat in the window of the boutique dressed in a costume to suit the theme of the day. Schiaparelli reports that he was soon married to Pascaline, who was "good and inconspicuous." Photographs show that while Pascal was indeed very handsome, Pascaline, like Edna Everage's sidekick, Madge, was markedly unglamorous. Although conventionally it is women rather than men who have been associated with beauty, Theodore Zeldin's examination of popular ideas about feminine appearance in the 1920s and 1930s reveals that male commentators implied, and also wrote, that most women were ugly, and that women clearly believed this (Zeldin 1973 Vol. 2: 440). Although women spent considerable sums on cosmetics and *coiffures* "the great attraction of fashion was that it diverted attention from the insoluble problems of beauty and provided an easy way—which money could buy—of at any rate approximating outwardly to a simply stated, easily reproduced, ideal of beauty" (1973 Vol. 2: 441). This is why, Zeldin argues, the "tyrants of fashion," the great designers of the period, were liberators too. Schiaparelli's clients, however, felt she liberated them from the banalities of 1930s fashions. One, Nadia Georges-Picot, interviewed years later, said: "she was much more than ... chiffons. Through costume she expressed a defiance of conventional aesthetics in a period where couture was losing itself in anaemic subtleties" (Musée de la Mode 1984: 125). The same client echoes the contrast between Pascal, the gorgeous peacock, and Pascaline, the dreary peahen, when talking about her husband, a well-known politician: "'I asked Schiap to make me the lamb chop hat. My husband was outraged, he didn't want to pay for it. I wore it all the same. Schiap's hats were such a 'concentrate' of chic and audacity . . . at that time men thought of themselves a bit like a pheasant, who drags the modest hen pheasant in his shadow" (1984: 123) In other words, within the supposedly "feminine" preoccupation with fashion lurked the audacity of the masquerade; in dressing *up* Pascal, and dressing *down* Pascaline, and then modeling themselves on Pascal, Schiaparelli and her clients recognized male privilege and then appropriated it to their own ends.

Pascal spent the war representing his country in the San Francisco Exhibition, leaning against a golden bicycle with a copy of *Paris-Soir* (which was changed daily) in his hand. He wore very chic Perugia cycling pumps, and a red, white and blue satin cyclist's outfit, including a blouse embroidered in diamonds with the words "Paris–San Francisco." After the war he came back to Paris and married Pascaline: "He looked at Pascaline with the disdain of a patriot and a world traveller, but Pascaline, who never had any brains, was merely panting to be back in his arms. The marriage was performed with pomp and champagne, after which normal life was re-established" (Schiaparelli 1954: 177–8).

The tendency to make-believe in Schiaparelli's autobiography, *Shocking Life*, makes it not unlike Claude Cahun's deconstructive autobiography of 1930, *Aveux Non Avenus* ("Disavowed Confessions" or "Voided Confessions"), where the narrative rapidly disintegrates from diary format to "aphorisms, dream sequences, imaginary dialogues and encounters" (Monahan 1995: 128). While Schiaparelli's book is ostensibly more commercial, and more mainstream, it is nevertheless playful and puzzling, full of distancing devices that serve to highlight the contingent and precarious nature of identity. For example, she refers to herself in both the first and third persons, switching at random; the Seine and the Eiffel Tower are personified, with human feelings and gestures attributed to them (The Eiffel Tower "looks down with surprise and sadness . . . the Seine was getting dressed up and ready for another great exhibition" (Schiaparelli 1954: 78)). Into her narratives she weaves tales of dummies and mannequins as if they were real people. We learn, for example, of the only horizontal fitting in the history of couture: "Mae West came to Paris. She was stretched out on the operating table of my workroom, and was measured and probed with care and curiosity" (1954: 95). The figure, however, turns out to be not Mae West, who was unable to attend a fitting in person, but a life-size model of her, posed naked as the Venus de Milo, which she had had made and sent to Paris from Hollywood. Schiaparelli very soon put the dummy to use in her *boutique*, where it stood in the window, and she also used it as the prototype for her "Shocking" perfume bottle, designed by Leonor Fini in 1937.

The figures of Pascal and Mae West testify to the passion for mannequins that Schiaparelli shared with the Surrealist artists. When invited to exhibit in the *Pavillon d'Elégance* at the 1937 Paris *Exposition*

Internationale (the one for which the Seine got dressed up) she intended to use Pascal. This was prohibited by the *Chambre Syndicale de la Couture Parisienne*, and so, disliking the conventional plaster mannequin provided, she created a Surrealist tableau by arranging the naked dummy on the ground, partially covered with flowers. She hung the mannequin's floral evening dress, underwear, stockings and shoes on a washing line nearby. A guest left a calling card with the mannequin expressing his condolences (R. Martin 1988: 56). The following year Schiaparelli attended the opening of the *1938 Exposition Internationale du Surréalisme*, in company with Bettina Bergery and Christian Bérard, the illustrator who illustrated many of her clothes in this period (Wilson 1938: 144). It was so crowded that the police closed the entrance for a short period; the decorator Jean-Michel Frank opened his shop next door, where those awaiting admission could view a lip-shaped Dalí sofa like one in Schiaparelli's salon (Altshuler 1994: 124).

The 1938 exhibition echoed Schiaparelli's mannequin display of the previous year in its recreation of a fictitious city street, the Rue Surréaliste, in which seventeen mannequins were arranged along its route, each with a fictitious Parisian street sign behind it and each adorned by an artist. Dalí's wore a Schiaparelli hat underneath a penguin's head and a scattering of small spoons over her torso. For the opening the hall was dark, and viewers had to rent a flashlight to look at the mannequins; as a result they "moved in a twilight realm, alluding to solicitation" (Belton 1995: 111). The ambiguous connection between the prostitute, the mannequin and the woman of fashion cannot be missed; the street sign above Marcel Duchamp's was Rue aux Lèvres, a pun on *rouge à lèvres*. Many other works exhibited made links with fashion, such as: Kurt Seligman's *Ultrameuble*, a stool with three legs in pink stockings and pink and black shoes; Marcel Jean's *Horoscope*, a dressmaker's dummy painted like a globe, the skeleton forming the land masses; Meret Oppenheim's fur-covered cup, saucer and spoon, *Petit déjeuner en fourrure*, of 1936, which was inspired by the fur-lined bracelets she made for Schiaparelli; and, in the lobby, Dalí's *Rainy Taxi* of 1938, a piece that, Schiaparelli-like, used mannequins as characters in a charade.

Schiaparelli was not included as an exhibitor in the 1938 *Exposition Internationale du Surréalisme*, even though her work had so much in common with the participating artists. Although cross-currents and similarities between the worlds of art and fashion in the late 1930s can be plotted, the two worlds did not entirely coalesce.[3] Nevertheless their paths crossed, both geographically and socially, in the fashionable spaces of Parisian social life of the late 1920s and 1930s. Bohemian social and sexual practices, in the form of Surrealist parties and masquerades, shared a common territory with the fashion in 1930s high society for extravagantly conceived costume balls. Both in the elaborately staged set-pieces of the latter, and in the avant-garde experimentation with gender and identity of the former, the performative and contingent roles of dress in the modern age are endlessly at play.

Parties

Schiaparelli had moved in Surrealist circles since the 1920s. She was a friend and colleague to a range of artists, but she also moved, both professionally and personally, in smart society. Although social distinctions were still maintained on both sides, in the 1920s and 1930s there was more fluidity between these social groups. In the 1920s the couturier Doucet paid André Breton and Louis Aragon to report to him on avant-garde painting and literature respectively. Both worlds met in *Le Boeuf sur le Toit*, the fashionable nightclub frequented by Aragon and Breton and also by the aristocratic Étienne de Beaumont.

The concepts of masquerade and the decentered self may also be set against the context of the increasing social fluidity of the inter-war years. The couturier Paul Poiret designed several great themed parties for himself either side of the First World War, and in the 1920s Chanel was among the first designers who began to move in the same social circles as their clients. In the 1930s Schiaparelli was a neighbor, friend and often hostess to her principal clients. Bettina Bergery was married to a diplomat, yet she worked as Schiaparelli's assistant, and Schiaparelli both designed for, and attended as a guest, many of her clients' costume balls, such as Daisy Fellowes' Oriental Ball in 1935, *Une soirée chez le Gouverneur*, to which Schiaparelli went as a black Venetian page. The same year as Schiaparelli's Circus collection Lady Mendl, another client of hers, gave a "circus" party. In 1939 the photographer André Durst gave a *Bal de la Forêt*, or "Night in the Forest," one of the last great costume balls of the decade. Schiaparelli was dressed as a Surrealist oak; Chanel dared her to dance with her and then steered her into some candles, where the tree caught fire (White 1986: 92). The Count Étienne de Beaumont, an "impresario of fashionable entertainment" (Haslam 1978: 73) devised an elaborate series of masquerade and costume balls in the 1930s known, in French, as *travestis*; for these Schiaparelli designed many of the costumes, and she attended several herself. (Dalí was also commissioned to do costumes for some balls, and the artists Jean Cocteau, Marie Laurencin and José-Maria Sert also designed balls for him.) One of the last was "At Court in Racine's Time," to which Schiaparelli was accompanied by her daughter Gogo dressed as the Ambassador of Siam.

Throughout all these festivities of the 1930s moved Schiaparelli, fusing her social and professional ties, and establishing the melancholic masquerade at the heart of the costume ball. The balls of the 1930s were meticulously plotted, and carefully rehearsed beforehand, down to gestures and items of dress (Cronin 1994: 27; Gold and Fizdale 1980:

239). A Man Ray photograph of *c. 1930* shows the Marchesa Casati at a de Beaumont ball: she is posed against a circus backdrop, and this, combined with the animal quality of her dress, is highly suggestive of Schiaparelli's design motifs. The Marchesa Casati, like Schiaparelli, crossed over socially between smart French society and the more bohemian art world. She is a pivotal figure because she was one of Schiaparelli's clients, and wore her masquerading fashions in both spheres. Another Man Ray photograph of 1932 shows Schiaparelli herself dressed in a long white dress decorated in white cocks' feathers for a White Ball of 1932.

Surrealist parties, by contrast to society balls, were less staged but equally extravagant. A famous Man Ray photograph of 1929 shows a ball at the Chateau of the Vicomte de Noailles. A sea motif prevailed at this costume ball held at the Noailles villa during the filming of *Les Mystères du Chateau du Dé* by Man Ray, who is lying down in the foreground. A year later he photographed Marie-Laure, the Vicomtesse de Noailles, in fancy dress as a squid. By 1932 the de Noailles were sponsoring Dalí and Cocteau, who both subsequently worked with Schiaparelli. Many other photographs bear witness to the exuberance of Surrealist parties and costumes:

> [Lee] Miller came to Surrealist parties displaying green fingernails and the gold handcuffs that Roland Penrose had given her . . . [Dorothea] Tanning adopted a leopard-skin costume covered with breasts. Among the many Surrealist accounts of festive gatherings is Julien Levy's description of a party organized by Tzara for which the guests were instructed to appear nude only from chest to thigh, and to which [Leonor] Fini wore knee-length white leatherette boots and a cape of white feathers and [Max] Ernst a belt of iron spikes, a headdress and breastplate made from pot scrubbers, and sandals with gray wings attached to them (Chadwick 1985: 106).

The guests nude from chest to thigh recall Schiaparelli's reversals, a 1934 hat with a veil that covered the mouth but left the eyes exposed, and an evening dress from the 1950s that covered the cleavage and dipped to reveal the upper part of the breasts. Among the male Surrealists many pictures of Marcel Duchamps, Tristan Tzara and especially Man Ray show that for men the pleasures of dressing up included those of cross-dressing.

The huge popularity in the 1930s of masquerade parties and balls is testimony not only to the influence of popular Surrealism on fashion and social life but also to a contemporary concern with the surface of things. Schiaparelli's designs, and the fashion for masquerade balls of the 1930s, as well as Surrealist publications, parties and manifestos, can all be taken as a response to, but also a participation in, a growing sense of the instability of the modern world. It is important finally to track this sense of instability to the international politics of the late 1930s.

Lights Out

In addition to changing ideas about the self, the map of Europe was shifting politically in the 1930s; Germany, Italy and Spain in their different ways lurched to the Right. The First World War had already shaken the foundations of many European beliefs and values. In France in particular parliamentary democracy had been discredited during the inter-war years by both left and right (Dean 1992: 224). And as the 1930s progressed, the threat of war loomed, however much some chose to ignore it. Malcolm Haslam describes the period from 1935 to the outbreak of war as one of "eerie gloom ... not a depressive gloom because Europe continued to glitter, despite economic problems and the threat of war" (Haslam 1978: 237). He argues that French society concentrated harder on concealing its knowledge of the disaster to come than on averting the catastrophe. In this period Schiaparelli's designs became more rather than less theatrical; she drew "the fancy dress and masquerade balls out of private mansions and onto the street" (R. Martin 1988: 172).

In 1938 Schiaparelli, who had started giving each collection a theme in 1935, exceeded herself and staged four remarkable fashion shows: in February she showed the Circus collection (Figure 2), in April the Pagan collection, in August the Astrology collection, and in October the *Commedia dell'arte* collection. The Circus collection show was particularly spectacular. Performers skipped up and down the staircase of her Place Vendôme showroom, jumped on and off the *vendeuses'* desks and in and out of the windows overlooking Napoleon's column by means of a ladder propped against the Louis XIV façade. In March Hitler's armies occupied Austria; the feeling of threat extended through 1938. The euphoria of Schiaparelli's Circus collection was succeeded by the darkly elegiac melancholy of the *Commedia dell'arte* collection, shown late in 1938, which was produced in a deteriorating political situation. Accompanied by the music of Scarlatti, Vivaldi, Pergolesi and Cimarosa, the show started with a harlequin dressed in a suit of half Hudson seal, half black wool, who was followed by other *commedia* characters: Columbine, Pedrolino (from Pierrot) and a troupe of *comédiennes*.

The following year, during the summer of 1939, Schiaparelli's window in the Place Vendôme displayed a large globe of the world with a dove sitting on it, an olive branch in its beak. But on 1 September 1939, Germany invaded Poland and France mobilized. Richard Martin analyzes Schiaparelli's work of the late 1930s as pure escapism: he says she was "at her most irrepressible at a time when Nazi rallies were supplanting circuses," and "as Europe headed towards war, Schiaparelli went to the circus" (Martin 1988: 198). While I do not entirely disagree, I would like tentatively to suggest that the argument may be more complex, perhaps as complex as Lou Taylor's discussion, in her study of Paris couture under the German occupation, of what, exactly, constitutes collaboration.[4]

Did Schiaparelli fiddle while Rome burned? Do her masquerading fashions of the 1930s amount to an avoidance of, even a denial of, social and political reality, a reality that includes inflation, unemployment, the rise of fascism? Or does her work indicate a deeper politics, a politics of identity, of a subjectivity that is split, alienated and constituted in language, an identity whose coherence is precarious and for which the "real self" that could be supposed to exist behind the mask recedes ever further, as in a hall of mirrors? Is Schiaparelli's witty play on the surface of bodies truly superficial, or truly profound, dealing with a politics that speaks to us today, the politics of subjectivity?

How, finally, should a dress designer respond to the rise of fascism? Chanel's functional, modernist designs, so clearly associated with the emancipation of women in the early twentieth century, could never be accused of escapism. Yet Chanel herself was anti-Semitic and a collaborator (Gold and Fizdale 1980: 288, 292, 296, 301–2; Haedrich 1972: 139, 144, 146–54, 192) where Schiaparelli, was liberal and anti-Fascist. Chanel's treatment of her workforce was harsh, whereas Schiaparelli, although described by some contemporaries as "difficult," was, by the standards of her day, a fair employer who paid her staff well. But to return to Schiaparelli's designs, perhaps her achievement *was* a political engagement, but of a sort that is only designated as political nowadays: the interrogation of the fundamental tropes of femininity via a playful and deconstructive appropriation of the stratagems of masquerade and performativity.

Notes

1. Lacan's concept of the Mirror Stage was first articulated in an unpublished conference paper given at Marienbad in 1936; it was reiterated in his 1938 article on the family in the *Encyclopédie Française*. The Marienbad paper was given again, in a revised form, in Zurich in 1949; it appeared in print in France in Lacan's *Écrits* in 1966, and is translated as 'The Mirror Stage as Formative of the Function of the I' in Lacan 1977: 1–7.
2. See "The Signification of the Phallus," in Lacan 1977: 281–91. The reference to comedy is on page 290. There is another translation, called "The Meaning of the Phallus," in Mitchell and Rose 1982: 74–85. Although Lacan's article was first presented in 1958 both Malcolm Bowie and Carolyn Dean argue that Lacan's writings of

the 1950s (which contain the references to masquerade) have their origins in his writings from the 1930s. Both cite, in particular, his article on the Papin sisters published in *Minotaure* in 1933 and the extended discussion of the female patient Aimée in his doctoral dissertation, published in 1932.

3. Richard Martin argues that art and fashion came close in this period as the Surrealist artists embraced disciplines related to fashion (R. Martin 1988: 50). It does not follow, however, that all the artists were in sympathy with the world of fashion, however drawn they were to its artefacts. Of the three organizers of the exhibition (Paul Eluard, André Breton and Marcel Duchamp) Breton was notably hostile to fashion and to smart society while Duchamp appears simply to have been indifferent to it. The exhibition did include the work of Dalí, Schiaparelli's closest Surrealist collaborator, but Breton was ambivalent about Dalí, nicknaming him 'Avida Dollars' (an anagram of Salvador Dalí). Dalí had been censured by the Surrealists in 1934 for his ambivalent attitude to Hitler, and in 1939 was excluded from the group. The work of Cocteau, Schiaparelli's other important collaborator, was considered slight and thin by Breton, who disliked his associations with *les snobs*. It was initially only through Louis Aragon that the Surrealists had a connection to Schiaparelli. Aragon was more dandyish than the other Surrealists, and he sometimes dressed in rubber gloves and played tricks on young women looking in the window of the jewelers Van Cleef & Arpel (Haslam 1978: 113). Described by contemporaries as elegant and charming, for years he sold jewelry made by his wife Elsa Triolet to the couture houses of Molyneux, Chanel and Schiaparelli (1978: 202). Together they designed an Aspirin Bracelet for Schiaparelli. Her assistant, Bettina Bergery, bought from Aragon, and little by little introduced other Surrealists to Schiaparelli (1978: 244–5). Other artists who made accessories for her were Leonor Fini and Meret Oppenheim.

4. See Lou Taylor, "Paris Couture 1940–44" in Juliet Ash and Elizabeth Wilson (eds). 1992. *Chic Thrills*. London: Pandora.

References

Altshuler, Bruce. 1994. *The Avant-Garde in Exhibition: New Art in the Twentieth Century*. New York: Harry N. Abrams.

Anderson, Mark M. 1992. *Kafka's Clothes: Ornament and Aestheticism in the Habsburg Fin de Siècle*. Oxford: Clarendon Press.

Augé, Marc. 1996. *Paris Années 30: Roger-Viollet*. Paris: Editions Hazan.

Bate, David (ed.) 1994. *Mise en Scène: Claude Cahun, Tacita Dean, Virginia Nimarkoh*. London: ICA.

Belton, Robert J. 1995. *The Beribboned Bomb: The Image of Woman in Male Surrealist Art*. Calgary: University of Calgary Press.

Benjamin, Walter. 1992. *One Way Street and Other Writings*, trans. Edmund Jephcott and Kingsley Shorter. London: Verso.

Bertin, Célia. 1956. *Paris à la Mode: A Voyage of Discovery*, trans. Marjorie Deans. London: Victor Gollancz.

Bowie, Malcolm. 1991. *Lacan*. London: Fontana.

Brandon, Ruth. 1990. *The New Woman and the Old Men: Love, Sex and the Woman Question*. London: Secker & Warburg.

Burgin, Victor *et al.* (eds) 1986. *Formations of Fantasy*. London and New York: Methuen. (Contains Joan Rivière, "Womanliness as a Masquerade," originally delivered 1929, at pp. 35–44; and also Stephen Heath, "Joan Rivière and the Masquerade.")

Butler, Judith. 1990. *Gender Trouble: Feminism and the Subversion of Identity*. London and New York: Routledge.

Caws, Mary Anne *et al.* (ed). 1991. *Surrealism and Women*. Cambridge, MA and London: MIT Press.

Chadwick, Whitney. 1985. *Women Artists and the Surrealist Movement*. London: Thames & Hudson.

Cronin, Vincent. 1994. *Paris: City of Light 1919–1939*. London: Harper Collins.

Dean, Carolyn J. 1992. *The Self and Its Pleasures: Bataille, Lacan and the History of the Decentered Subject*. Ithaca, NY and London: Cornell University Press.

Doane, Mary Ann. 1982. "Film and the Masquerade: Theorizing the Female Spectator." *Screen*, Vol. 23, No. 3–4, Sept.–Oct., 74–87.

——. 1988/89. "Masquerade Reconsidered: Further Thoughts on the Female Spectator." *Discourse*, 11, Fall/Winter: 42–54.

Éditions Paris-Musées. 1987. *Paris Couture Années trente*. Paris: Société de l'histoire de costume.

Evans, Caroline and Minna Thornton. 1989. *Women and Fashion: A New Look*. London: Quartet Books.

Flanner, Janet. 1932. "The Comet: Elsa Schiaparelli." *New Yorker*.

Gold, Arthur and Robert Fizdale. 1980. *Misia: The Life of Misia Sert*. London: Macmillan.

Haedrich, Marcel. 1972. *Coco Chanel: Her Life, Her Secrets*, trans. Charles Lam Markmann. London: Hale.

Haslam, Malcolm. 1978. *The Real World of the Surrealists*. London: Weidenfeld & Nicolson.

Kotz, Liz. 1992. Interview with Judith Butler. *Artforum*. November.

Lacan, Jacques. 1977. *Écrits*, trans. Alan Sheridan. London: Tavistock.

Lasalle, Honor and Abigail Solomon-Godeau. 1992. "Surrealist Confession: Claude Cahun's Photomontages." *Afterimage*, Vol. 19, March: 10–13.

Leperlier, François. 1992. *Claude Cahun: l'écart et la métamorphose*. Paris: Jean-Michel Place.

Lévi-Strauss, Claude. 1982. *The Way of the Masks*, trans. Sylvia Modleski. University of Washington Press.

Lichtenstein, Therese. 1992. "A Mutable Mirror: Claude Cahun." *Artforum*, Vol. 19, pt. 8, April: 64–7.

Liebemann, Lisa. 1988. "Fetishes and feints." *Artscribe International* (UK), No. 69, May: 42–45.

Martin, Jean-Hubert. 1982. *Man Ray: Photographe*, 2nd edition. Paris: Philippe Sers.

Martin, Richard. 1988. *Fashion and Surrealism*. London: Thames & Hudson.

Mitchell, Juliet and Jacqueline Rose (eds). 1982. *Feminine Sexuality: Jacques Lacan and the École Freudienne*, trans, Jacqueline Rose. London: Macmillan.

Monahan, Laurie J. 1995. "Radical Transformations: Claude Cahun and the Masquerade of Womanliness." In M. Catherine de Zegher (ed.), *Inside the Visible: An Elliptical Traverse of 20th Century Art*, pp. 125–33. Cambridge, MA and London: MIT Press.

Musée de la Mode. 1984. *Hommage à Elsa Schiaparelli*. Paris: Musée de la Mode.

Rajchman, John. 1986. "Lacan and the Ethics of Modernity." *Representations*, 15, Summer: 42–56.

Schiaparelli, Elsa. 1954. *Shocking Life*. London: Dent.

Sobieszek, Robert and Deborah Irmas. 1994. *the camera i*. Los Angeles: Los Angeles Museum of Art and Harry N. Abrams.

Steele, Valerie, 1988. *Paris Fashion: A Cultural History*. New York and Oxford: Oxford University Press.

Stuart, Andrea. 1996. *Showgirls*. London: Cape.

Tardiff, Richard D. and Lothar Schirmer (eds). 1991. *Horst: Sixty Years of Photography*. London: Thames & Hudson.

Taylor, Lou. 1992. "Paris Couture 1940–44." In Juliet Ash and Elizabeth Wilson (eds), *Chic Thrills*. London: Pandora.

Tseëlon, Effrat. 1995. *The Masque of Femininity: The Presentation of Woman in Everyday Life*. London, Thousand Oaks and New Delhi: Sage.

Vertès. 1935. "De Fêtes en Fêtes." *Vogue*, Paris, 26 August.

White, Palmer. 1986. *Elsa Schiaparelli: Empress of Fashion*, with a foreword by Yves Saint Laurent. London: Aurum Press.

——. 1994. *Haute Couture Embroidery: The Art of Lesage*. Berkeley, CA: Lacis.

Wilson, Bettina. 1938. "Surrealism in Paris." *Vogue*, USA, 1 March.

Zeldin, Theodore. 1973. *A History of French Passions, 1848–1945: Volume One: Ambition, Love and Politics; Volume 2: Intellect, Taste and Anxiety*. Oxford: Clarendon Press.

Fashion Theory, Volume 3, Issue 1, pp.33–50
Reprints available directly from the Publishers.
Photocopying permitted by licence only.
© 1999 Berg. Printed in the United Kingdom.

Transvesty— Travesty: Fashion and Gender[1]

Barbara Vinken

Barbara Vinken is a Professor of French and Comparative Literature, currently visiting at Humboldt Universität, Berlin. In addition to her scholarly work in Renaissance, 18th and 19th century literature, she has written a book on fashion, *Mode nach der Mode: Geist und Kleid am Ende des Jahrhunderts* (Frankfurt am Main: Fischer 1993) and edited a book on pornography, *Die nackte Wahrheit* (München: DTV 1997). She has just finished a book on *The German Mother* (München: Piper 2000).

Fashion is a phenomenon of the modern. It emerges in the second half of the nineteenth century as a post-feudal phenomenon. Previously, to put the matter in simplified terms, there had been dress codes, the sense and purpose of which had been the meticulous and even cavilling representation of gender and class through an established code. The type of fur, the width of the authorized velvet collars, and the quantity of pleats, for instance, distinguished nobility from non-nobility and determined standing in a class society. Clothes were intended to indicate at a single glance just who it was one was confronted with. They were supposed to guarantee and establish social readability. Because it was so tempting and also in a certain sense so easy to appear as someone other than who one really was, specific dress codes were never maintained for very long. In a condition of permanent violation there was need of constant admonition and the firmest threats, which led to a flood of decrees. In an order of representation guaranteed in this manner by clothing it could truly be said that clothes "made" people.

From the very beginning, fashion has disrupted this order of representation. It exposes each representation as a distortion. Its particular point resides in this disruption; this is what turns it into fashion. This specific trait of fashion has been largely overlooked or repressed in sociological analyses of fashion. Sociological discourse on fashion has tried to turn fashion into precisely that which it is not. In sociology, fashion is treated as a mode of representation. It represents, accordingly, nothing but class and gender, albeit with greater difficulty than was the case in times of the established code. Because hierarchical orders are suspended in democracies, because everyone is equal and no one can be told what to wear, the lower classes imitated the upper classes as their "reference group." Fashion, as sociology suggests unison, follows the law of the *trickle-down effect* from the top down. The need for distinction, the need to show who one is (Bourdieu: 1979, 258–60), and above all to distinguish oneself from the lower classes, leads to a breathtakingly rapid transition, which—very obviously—distinguishes fashion from dress codes (Simmel 1919: 44). To follow sociologists, it is the most exclusive task of fashion, almost its motor, to guarantee that in increasingly unclear circumstances clothing adequately represents gender and, above all, class.

In crass contradiction to this thesis stands the fact that since the beginning of *haute couture* fashion can only adequately be described as cross-dressing. Fashion is, at the risk of overstating the case, masquerade: transvestism, travesty. This is certainly not to suggest, at least not without further qualification, that fashion represents a category, gender, that sociology simply left uninterrogated. That it also represents class in this highly paradoxical manner and at the expense of a marked sexuality was, contrary to the claims of the sociologists, a fact that was not to be overlooked in the world of fashion. It was precisely the *grande bourgeoise* who searched for "new ideas in the cesspool of the Parisian demi-monde," as the sociology of fashion acknowledged in its shock (von Ihering 1883: 236; Benjamin 1983, 125). Does fashion travel from the bottom up after all? In any event fashion threw to the wind an opposition that had been central for the feminine world of the nineteenth century, the opposition between the decent woman and the coquette, so that Friedrich Theodor Vischer very early on and with great verve lamented the erotic problems presented by clothing (Vischer 1879). These findings are shared by two novelists who seem to be linked by little else, Zola and Proust. Egon Friedell's astute description of the new fashion category of the "grande dame, who plays the coquette," supports the idea that the category of representation has been drawn too narrowly

(Friedell 1931: 203; Benjamin 1983: 125). Through fashion, class and gender enter into an intimate relationship that cannot be grasped by the more or less unequivocal and clear claims of representational classification.

To illuminate these complications, I would like to try to look back on the hour of fashion's birth. It was Georg Simmel who described fashion as a post-feudal phenomenon. This is significantly more accurate than characterizing it as a bourgeois phenomenon. While it cannot be separated from the rise of the bourgeoisie, fashion is a strangely marginalized, anti-bourgeois enclave within bourgeois society, which in its association with the feminine and the aristocratic draws their respective spheres together. The association of aristocracy, femininity and appearance was already a commonplace of the Enlightenment, which posited the pure republic against so much triviality: against the corrupt, weak, effeminate monarchy rose up a masculine republic sworn to virtue. It is characterized by an unaffected strictness and, in addition to freedom, equality and fraternity, also promotes the disappearance of everything feminine from the public sphere (Vinken 1995). Precisely this ideology dominates postrevolutionary French society and all modern democracies.

In the age of the bourgeoisie, the world of fashion—which is often the world of the *demi-monde*—strangely enough parodies the world of the nobility. Charles Frederick Worth, the first name in fashion and thus the first fashion designer in the contemporary sense of the word, reigned like an absolute monarch—but only over ladies of society, whom he ruled according to the whim of his genius in complete disregard of their social rank. His omnipotence is simultaneously his impotence; as the ruler of the disenfranchized, he becomes a parody of a ruler. His masculinity is quickly called into question. The more securely women are excluded from the sphere of power and authority that is divided up among men, the more generously the attributes of nobility are distributed among them: they are elevated to the status of absolute ruler over their men, queen of hearts, tyrannical mistress, whose least whim is yielded to and at whose feet everything is willingly laid—everything, on condition that they remain completely powerless.

Bourgeois man—and he is the only true man—stands in a certain negative relation to this world of frivolous appearance. He "is"—and needs therefore neither to represent nor to appear. The ability to identify oneself with the masculine leads to the standardization of male clothing, which oscillates between the most diverse sporting and business motifs. For in contrast to the masculine body of the court, the bourgeois masculine body is not sexually marked. Every masculine display of elegance is proscribed. The beauty of the male leg, the play of calf and thigh, which was distinguished to advantage in skin-tight, flesh-colored boots or embroidered silk stockings, the tone and coloring of the skin, whose snowy beauty was highlighted by sumptuous lace, the *braguette* or so-called codpiece, which was set off from the legs, and in size, ornamentation and exaggerating realism left nothing to be desired—all the ornaments of masculinity come to an end with the new drainpipe trousers. The nineteenth century was characterized as the century of "masculine renunciation" (Flugel 1930, 110 ff.). To the extent to which he renounces fashion and indulges in the, in the truest sense of the word, simplistic rhetoric of anti-rhetoric, what man gains thereby is in no way insignificant: identity, authenticity, unquestioned masculinity, seriousness.

To be sure, it comes even here to a characteristic non-simultaneity of the simultaneous. The court brings noble, representative masculinity as a historical surplus and relic from a bygone age into civilian uniforms whose splendor now seems more like a curiosity. Upon the occasion of an exhibition of the wardrobe of the Viennese court from the time of Sissi and Franz-Josef, *Figaro Magazine* emphasized the magnificence of the parade uniforms. Richly embroidered, studded with pearls, turquoise and silver, and lined with mink and panther, they were equal in their splendor to the women's robes. These uniforms are relics from the imperial, and in the strictest sense the premodern and prefashionable, non-bourgeois period, which in their aggressive withdrawal from modern life represent a peculiar outlet of suppressed tendencies. In a constant state of exception in bourgeois times, the uniformed man marks a masculine sexuality that is not particularly emphasized by the bourgeois suit. In opposition to the dandy or the woman, this masculinity that is uniformly marked by the uniform does not bear the stamp of the aristocratic-feminine or the heroic-solitary, which is completely wrapped up in frivolity and ostentatiously resists all functionalization, but rather the stamp of a strictly hierarchized and functionalizable collectivity. In themselves premodern phenomena, uniforms, owing to their massive presence in bourgeois society, assume a unique status by representing the only place where masculinity is literally "on parade." At least until its achievement after the two world wars of the perfection of the camouflage-uniform according to the ideal of the guerilla, the uniform maintained something of the display of splendor of the nobility.

It is the uniform's uniform suitability for the masses that has enabled its reappearance in the fashion of the modern. The body that was first standardized and measured was the body of the soldier in the Prussian army. The military's norming and standardization of the human body according to sizes—still four at that time, the so-called stomach sizes of the officers not included—is the *sine qua non* of the *prêt-à-porter* (Mentges 1995: 42). Modern fashion is thus to a certain extent tailored after the uniform.

Beyond the technical measure that was provided by the uniformity of uniforms, uniforms offered a wealth of references as diverse as they were puzzling—from the blue admiral's jacket with gold buttons and gold stripes on the arm, combined with white pants for both men and women, all the way to the martial uniform-rags in the fashion of Gaultier. Within the masculine-homosexual spectrum, the quasi-uniformed, ultramacho men—culminating in Tom's men—form the counterpart to queens and fairies; they constantly and permanently stress that one can be queer without being feminine; rather one can be a complete man, a real man, more masculine than other men. This ostentation of the more masculine, this excess of staging and presentation, this "having too much" and "being more" awakens the suspicion that one is perhaps really not, that one does not actually have.

The bourgeois man who renounces all sexuality that is marked by his clothes is able to escape this threat. Clothing never divided the sexes more rigidly than in the nineteenth century. Not only did men and women clothe themselves very differently; it was above all the relationship of clothing to gender that was different—with the strange exceptions of the dandy and the uniform. The masculine was the unmarked gender; the feminine on the other hand was the marked sexuality. "His" eternally inconspicuous dark suit provides the ideal matt background before which "she" can really spring into life with the brilliance of silk, the sparkle of jewels, the shimmer of naked skin and the ivory of the *décolletée*. The affluence of the man highlighted in charcoal gray cloth and left in understatement finds in the jewel at his side an object of display floating in silks and furs, hung with jewelry and dazzling in bright colors. Thorstein Veblen characterized the woman of the nineteenth century for this reason as *mobilia*, as the mobile property of her husband (Veblen 1965[1899]). Her function consisted in exhibiting his fortune: her appearance, his being (*ihr Schein, sein Sein*). "She" represents his fortune in the opulence of her clothes, in the rapid transitions of fashion, but also in a body that in its clothing exhibits its unsuitability for work and announces that it is well maintained. Fashion and femininity have become synonymous.[2]

Just how completely this purely historical alignment of femininity and marked sexuality *qua* fashion versus masculinity and unmarked sexuality *qua* indifference to fashion has become the most natural thing in the world and has virtually attained the status of an anthropological given is demonstrated in the description that Richard Alewyn has given of aristocratic men's fashion of the seventeenth and eighteenth centuries. Colorful, resplendent, richly ornamented with ribbons, bows, lace and feathers, studded with pearls, precious stones and valuable buttons, and embroidered with gold, the clothing of the masculine nobility at the court of Louis XIV appears "effeminate" to him: the man decorated himself, as the woman did, in order to be an ornament. Like her, his status at court is determined by appearance. Exactly in the tradition of republican discourse, Alewyn attributes this confusion of spheres to the nobility's loss of power. Since the nobility was no longer what it once had been, nothing else remained for it but to appear in this way (Alewyn and Salzle 1959: 36 ff.). The man of the eighteenth century, the man of court, who did not yet appear as earnestly unrefined as his bourgeois successor, but was instead equal to the ladies of the court in gracefulness and elegance, was not seen as a real man in the age of the bourgeoisie, but rather as effeminate and grovelling.[3] Such argumentation completely overlooks the fact that the feudal nobility of the Renaissance, which also clothed itself no less magnificently than did its courtly successors, remains immune to any argument based on deprivation of power. One thinks of the tight velvet trousers, the full feathered hats, the expensively embroidered jerkins of velvet and silk and the colorful and diverse patterns of the codpieces. This view decodes the epoch before the historical shift according to the standards of our contemporary codes of gender and representation. Lacan's dictum that the parade of the masculine, the display of masculinity, appears effeminate is as correct for the bourgeois epoch as it is false for the feudal epoch.

Hence, in reference to gender relations, we find ourselves in the bourgeois period, if not in a completely new situation, then at least in a radicalized one. The boundary that constitutes society no longer divides the noble from the non-noble, but rather the feminine from the masculine. The opposition feminine/masculine is doubled, however, by a second opposition, that of noble and bourgeois, in which case "noble" had become a metaphor for the appearance of power. To bring the matter to a point, the bourgeoisie uses its women to exhibit the castration of the nobility. The all-determining opposition that constitutes sexual difference is that of authentic and inauthentic. Men "are": they are someone, they are authentic, real; women on the other hand appear artificial, inauthentic. Fashion emerges as something that is excluded from the apparently non-rhetorical authenticity of the bourgeois masculine collective, because in drawing together femininity and nobility on the basis of their shared frivolity of appearance, it thus excluded them from the real world in which men remained and remain among themselves securely enclosed within the institutions of masculinity.

The reform movement in clothing that was supported by various parts of the suffragette movement attempted to eradicate this evil through a type of clothing that was intended to be "naturally" attractive to women. This clothing, which sought in the name of the natural to avoid any suggestion of the erotic, was intended to enable women to dissolve into the collective of men in unmarked sexuality. These efforts were not crowned with success. For it is true here as well that, in an opposition of two terms, the one, authenticity, remains dependent upon the other, inauthenticity, and that both terms function only in and as an oppositional relation. The inauthenticity of women is the necessary condition for the authenticity of men.

Formulating itself as a discourse in clothes about clothes, as a commentary in certain respects, fashion followed a direction that was the exact opposite of that taken by the reform movement in clothing. Rather than unmarked sexuality, it stressed marked sexuality at all costs. On the trail of the vicissitudes of desire, it can do nothing but mark sexuality as paradox. On the one side, it establishes the division of the genders "feminine"/"masculine"—that is to say, marked versus unmarked sexuality, "inauthentic" versus "authentic"—by making this division visible; at the same time, however, it disrupts this constitutive opposition. It is self-deconstructive in certain respects; it undermines what it constitutes. And it does so, according to my thesis, through hyperfetishization. Fashion is a fetishism of the second degree.

The first-degree fetishism of clothing becomes tangible in the female body, which is overstressed in its secondary sexual characteristics. This body is manifest in the roaring success of the wonder- and push-up-bra and the high sales of the bustle or padded girdle. Women are supposed to embody a norm that is simultaneously an ideal form, the schema of an ideal, standard-setting body. Fashion exhibits artificiality and inaccessibility precisely in this strived-for goal of embodying the ideal. If the bustle when worn by women is designed to increase their erotic appeal in the eyes of men, when worn by men it (as well as other types of padding) serves, according to findings of *Focus*, to emphasize, not their masculine appeal in the eyes of women, but rather their career potential. The padded female body refers to the fashions of the nineteenth century, which went to such extremes in the eroticization of the female body that hats were launched that provided instructions to those who could read them on how the crinoline was to be opened. While the male body almost disappeared beneath loosely fitting fabric, the silhouette of the female body was staged as a production in increasingly surface-intensive and spatially extensive terms (Musil 1978: 1193–8). The production of femininity was, and is becoming once more, a full-time job. Between diets, the gym, the hairdresser's, the beauty salon and shopping, the women in Cooker's film *Women* and Woody Allen's film *Alice* hardly have enough time left over to spin their intricate webs of intrigue, which all revolve around a hardly visible and completely inconspicuous husband. The heroine of *Clueless* not only spends exhausting days in the shopping mall; she also puts together her wardrobe by computer, and checks the effect by video camera. Like Cooker's women before her, she is a heroine of manipulation. As a branch of production, femininity does not remain a privilege of the upper class. On the contrary, it facilitates the possibility of tearing down class distinctions. Frederick's of Hollywood, whose catalogs supplied American women for over twenty years with padding, supports, and bindings of all kinds, with corsages, satin nightgowns and sexy lace underwear, very early on conceived of this disruption of the structure of class relations—which in French novels appears more as a pheno-menon of unrest—in terms of its American democratic potential: he wanted to use sexiness as a means of providing all women with equal opportunity—not in relation to men, of course, but rather in the eyes of men (Gottwald and Gottwald 1970: 9).

Fetishism is in the air; one could almost speak at present of a fetishization of fetishism. If my description of the fashion of the modern depends upon the concept of the fetish, this is due to the fact that in fashion the fetish arrives at its ancestral realm: the realm of the stuff of which dreams are made, the realm of accessories. The structure that determines the fetish—the oscillation between the animate and the inanimate—is unceasingly staged in fashion. What is artificial becomes naturalized, what is natural becomes artificial. Already in its etymological sense of "making, producing, manufacturing," the fetish is a product of art, associated with artificiality, and thus the female body must also count as such a product of art. In this regard, make-up can be understood as a trace of the fetish after which the female body is modeled in the realm of fashion.

The fetish is not least an object to which magic powers are attributed in the transition from the organic to the inorganic: a dead though nevertheless strangely animated object whose artificial animation produces a kind of fascination that can petrify its spectator, blinded by the radiant shine of jewels; that captivates him in its enchantment, robs him of breath and places him under its spell. "*Idole*", writes Baudelaire in his *Éloge du maquillage*, "*elle doit se dorer pour etre adorée*" (Baudelaire 1962: 492). The moment of the shift of the animate into the inanimate, into the inanimate shine of adoration, is a constitutive element for fashion: the trophy of the dead animal on the living body, the mask of make-up on the living face, the precious gems that cover the body with minerals or, yet more radically, fashion's body as a doll's body set in motion, as the living body of a statue. This transformation of the doll, preferably Barbie, into a living woman and vice versa, or the oscillation between statue and living woman, determines fashion photography in the blink of an eye.

Fashion stages this transformation of the inorganic into the organic. This is, following Benjamin, the secret at the heart of the fashion of the modern: "There is in every fashion something of a bitter satire of love, in every fashion perversions are imbedded in the most reckless manner. Every fashion is at war with the organic. Every fashion couples the living body to the inorganic world . . . Fetishism, which is based on the sex-appeal of the inorganic, is its vital nerve" (Benjamin 1983: 125).

If the concept of the fetish is allowed to slip over into the psycho-analytic register, then femininity becomes first and foremost a substitute. It stands for something else, for it does not refer to itself but rather to man: it stands for his wealth (*Vermögen*)—one recalls the wonderful ambiguity of the wealthy or potent (*vermögend*) man in Freud's analysis of Dora—or, as Veblen once said with a peculiar conciseness: it exhibits his wealth. He, who "is," represents himself through it. Paradoxically, the ideal femininity that is embodied in the real woman signifies "man." In contrast to her, only man is allowed the privilege of meaning, the privilege of a literal identity. That is the most profound reason that the feminine gender role is from the very outset a travesty, a masquerade of male identity (Felman 1981).

Ideal femininity, idealized femininity, femininity as it is supposed to "be," is determined by the sign of the masculine, which it has as its signified. The difference between the sexes is fixed in a hierarchized opposition that assigns to each of the two sexes an unequivocal place, and thereby secures sexual identity. This arrangement, which secures the principle of identity through the principle of opposition, functions at its core fetishistically: masculinity is complemented and brought to completion in relation to the difference of the sexes, or castration, which is threateningly inscribed within femininity, while castration is distorted and real sexual difference is thereby extinguished—not although, but rather precisely because, the woman is ideally consumed in her relation to the masculine. Only in so far as "she" is mere woman, can "he" be wholly man. She no longer appears as his mirror image—as castrated woman—but rather as the fascinating, beguiling object of desire: she "is" his wealth. Femininity is thus a masquerade, and his supposed being (*Sein*) is the product of her seeming (*Schein*).

In transvestism, the travesty of this travesty, the masquerade of this masquerade, resides the unspoken secret of *haute couture*, which accordingly has an affirmative, hyperfetishistic structure. As the travesty of a travesty, it exhibits the oppositionally secured, unequivocal identity of sex as the result of masquerade, and topples literal, unmarked masculinity.

To exhibit means either to mark or cancel the fetish that "femininity" is. Fashion does not represent the sexes, and therefore the alternative program to the marked or cancelled fetish of "femininity" cannot be the true, finally authentic woman. If it represents at all, fashion represents the unrepresentability of sexual difference, the impossibility, in other words, of *not* wearing a mask. It does so by completely and recklessly exploiting sexual difference, the oppositionally organized identity of social gender roles. Precisely through this unscrupulous bringing-into-play of the clichés of gender roles, the true woman and the real man do not emerge as reality, but rather as phantasma in a system of the sexes that has been fetishized and phallicized into pure identity. In drag, the gender role that drag is becomes visible to the precise extent that it completely affirms the object of desire, *femininity*, in its fetishization.

Fashion is—such was my original thesis—cross-dressing. Its star is, not by mere chance, the transvestite: "My most elegant clients," Christian Lacroix remarks, "are no longer women, but New York queens." The woman who is responsible for having fundamentally revolutionized European fashion and its attendant concept of femininity also appears in the name of the opposite sex: Rei Kawakubo keeps shop under the name of "Comme des Garçons" (Like [the] Boys). It would however be too easy to describe this cross-dressing, which fashion is, simply in terms of "man into woman" or "woman into man." In fashion, gender and class intersect. *Haute couture* dresses women not simply as normal men, but as dandies. Yet what has made the dandy into not just "fashion's beast of burden" (König 1974), but the first fashionable creature in the modern sense? First, that he is different from other men. Like a woman or an aristocrat, the dandy is too much and too noticeably concerned with his appearance. His relentless *pursuit of elegance*, his untiring pursuit of the most refined form and the perfect detail is not just an end in itself, but much more a protest against the authenticity of the bourgeois collective of men. He was defined against the backdrop of the aristocratic and the feminine, his heroism fanned by the *odor di femmina*. He was celebrated by Baudelaire as the "black prince of elegance." To the extent that as a man the dandy obviously placed all the value in the world on his clothing—so that he often went broke, even to the point of ruin—he not only eroticized his body but positioned himself within the context of pure seeming (*Schein*), which was ideologically foreign to bourgeois, masculine being (*Sein*). The related eroticization remains under the sign of the feminine.

What is it that structurally happens here? The classifications of male/unmarked/authentic and female/marked/inauthentic, so central for identity, which is to say for the opposition of masculine and feminine, are opened out. The dandy, a curiously inauthentic man, lets other men appear less authentically, less naturally masculine.

Haute couture derives its refinement and wit from just this rupture, from these dissonances. From its beginning, *haute couture* has been an adaptation of the fashion of the dandy for women, which would sometimes be lost without its orientalisms. It begins by disgarding feminine clothing altogether, with Paul Poiret's gesture of getting rid of the corset. With his long and extremely tight dresses, which gave the impression of a certain arabesque figure when worn, Poiret later prided himself on having robbed women once more, from below, of the freedom of movement that had come about owing to the absence of the corset. This sadism, which appeared in the guise of poetic justice, was calculated to conceal one of his greatest flops: namely, Poiret had in fact attempted in vain to introduce European women to the kind of pants that were worn in the Orient by both men and women, and thus to introduce not only total freedom of movement for the legs, but also the masculine article of clothing *par excellence* into women's fashion. That had not happened since the French Revolution, which prescribed by decree who wore the pants. The revolutionary decree, which established the order of the sexes in no uncertain terms, was declared law in the much celebrated Code Napoléon in order to return the "gendered beings which had gotten out of control" to their place and to set an end to their "most offensive lack of restraint" (Wolter 1995: 72). Even the exotic index of orientalism, which had taken the sting out of the masculine from the very outset, since the oriental *per se* stood in suspicious proximity to effeminacy, did not help Poiret and his pants.

The style of the dandy was definitively assimilated into *haute couture* by Coco Chanel, who facilitated its integration in every aspect. Marlene Dietrich's tuxedo, which Yves Saint Laurent introduced into *haute couture* in the seventies, represents the final link in a long chain of appropriations. Chanel, speaking of herself in the third person, is said to have confided to Salvador Dalí that "she took the English masculine and made it feminine. All her life, all she did was change men's clothing into women's: jackets, hair, neckties, wrists" (Parinaud 1981: 212). One easily recognizes that the godfather of this new femininity in the sign of the masculine was not the sexually unmarked, bourgeois man, but the dandy. This becomes apparent not because of the kind of appropriated clothing, but rather because of the manner in which this fashion is worn. The *désinvolture*, the nonchalance, the poverty *de luxe*, as Poiret indulging in oriental lavishness derisively called it—in short, the carefully cultivated appearance of not having invested any thought in the clothes that one wore—all this belongs to the credo of the perfect dandy.

Chanel's dandy fashion translates thereby another translation. It is the reappropriation of the previous appropriation by some few men of a fashion that had once been coded as feminine and aristocratic. Chanel translates this new "masculine" into women's fashion.

A different model of the overlapping of class and gender is represented by Dior, who clothed woman as femme/femme, as only woman, as wholly woman at last—and that means once again as unscrupulously artificial and hampered—supposedly, in other words, without the detour through the masculine. Interestingly, Coco Chanel had interpreted this detour through the masculine as "naturally" feminine. Chanel self-confidently maintained that she clothed real women for real life. While Chanel dressed woman as a dandy, Dior, with his ultrafeminized New Look, with the wasp-waist, the corset, full skirts and stiletto-heels, did not however succeed in transforming his clients into real women— as the relieved press, confronted with such captivating femininity, mistakenly supposed. Chanel, who reacted to this new fashion like a bull before a red flag, had a better sense of what was going on. She was of the opinion that Dior had dressed his clients up as transvestites. Beside herself with rage at this new direction in fashion, Chanel is supposed— at least according to the reports of her biographers—to have screeched: "look at them . . . dressed by queens living out their fantasies. They dream of being women, so they make real women look like transvestites" (Zeffirelli 1985: 100). Mrs Chanel attributed this *faux pas* to the fact that Dior naturally could not have known what a woman was, since he himself had never had one. We post-Lacanians, as it were, know better: we know that it does not help to have had a woman. Chanel's women— although she had had women and was a woman herself—were not more natural in the least, although they were perhaps more modern. And this, because they did not embody the type of the femme/femme but rather that of the *garçonne*—the natural woman, therefore?

Woman as dandy, woman as transvestite. In the early days of *haute couture*, woman most certainly embodied the fetish of femininity. This clear relation changes in the fashion of the eighties, which I have described as fashion after fashion (Vinken 1993). That does not mean that as a result the division between femininity and masculinity has grown less sharp; it does however have increasingly less to do with so-called biological gender. Four types emerge in fashion that had not previously existed. First, men can shine forth in the beguiling brilliance of the fetish of femininity: man as man as woman. This fashion very often no longer has anything idealizing about it, as had been the case for instance with Dior's femme/femme. Even if in Dior's ultrafemininity the sublime and the ridiculous are, to quote Napoleon, only a step apart, with Dior the scales clearly tip in the direction of sublimity and authentification. This is also true, by the way, of other ultrafetishistic designers, such as Montana, Mugler or Versace. With Gaultier, on the other hand, it moves rather in the direction of the ridiculous. His point of reference is no longer the *grande dame*, commanding the attention of everyone around her, nor even the merely charming girl next door, but rather the petty bourgeois woman who, eager to conform, bravely chases after the ideal of the dream woman and is all the more ridiculously helpless for her efforts. Weird and not pretty: this could be Gaultier's, and not just Gaultier's, motto.

Secondly, this fetish of femininity, having been appropriated by men, can be stolen and reappropriated once more—together with the inscribed traces of the first appropriation—by women—without however running the risk of authentification or naturalization. Third—and this is probably the most pure and formally refined type of fashion, which has been given the label of *deconstruction*—woman can carry fetishized femininity with her as a kind of mask or masquerade, exhibiting herself as a more or less unsuccessful embodiment. Fourth, woman emerges as an injured fetish, in whom the trace of castration has been registered. This is a type I can only hint at here, since it is less an expression of the clothing than a technique of fashion photography, most impressively illustrated by Richardson.

Before I come to Jean Paul Gaultier, who is perhaps the contemporary designer who most effectively, though perhaps not most subtly, carries out the dismantling of the fetish of femininity through woman, I would like to glance briefly at a Belgian designer from the Antwerp school, Martin Margiela. Margiela does not work primarily with cross-dressing; rather he has developed a strictly formal, and for fashion understood as a coded system perhaps more innovative and radical, procedure of exposing the difference between the fetish of femininity and woman. His fashion makes the body readable as a site of fetishistic inscriptions, precisely because it is not identical to these inscriptions, does not embody them, but rather bears fetishistic femininity as a construct foreign to it. This is achieved through a refined interaction between the tailor's dummy, in French *mannequin*, as the measure by which bodies are normed and to which all bodies are reduced, and the living body—between tailor's dummy and woman (Vinken 1997).

Margiela pulls the mannequin from out of the "obscene" beyond and into the spotlight of the stage. He dresses his women as mannequins, as tailor's dummies. His finished clothes appear as if they were still on the mannequin, pinned with tacking thread, the modelling pins and threads turned outward, visibly adorned with all the technical accoutrements of its production. They expose and turn inside out all the tricks of the tailor's trade that are otherwise so perfectly concealed. The art of tailoring consists in allowing the body of this dummy—embodied by women—to appear as nature. Named after the tailor's dummy—in Flemish *mannekin*, mannequins set the dummy's body in motion. Thus the perfect woman, if one follows the Flemish trace at the heart of French fashion, is—in purely etymological terms—a *manikin*, a little man not so much in the sense of a diminution, but in the sense rather of the—detachable—masculine sex: accessory. These "unfinished" clothes expose the hidden nexus of fashion as fascination with the inanimate, with the dummy or doll at their heart. In Margiela's work, this process is exposed and reversed: rather than the inanimate model's being being perfectly embodied, the living human body itself appears as *mannekin*; it appears in the form of a tailor's dummy. Woman is not herself inscribed with the fetish of femininity, but rather this fetish is presented as foreign—as a foreign body.

The loss of this fetishized femininity that is ideally embodied in woman is lamented in certain circles of fashion journalism as a disempowerment of woman; no one would be charmed or enraptured, *Le Monde* suggested in its criticism of the *Prêt-à-porter 96*, by mannequins dressed as paupers. That is, contemporary fashion seems less incapable than unwilling to send women out on to the catwalk who typify anything less than the perfect woman.

Gaultier achieves his effects, not like Margiela through a severely formal procedure that is immanent to *haute couture* itself, but rather through a massive staging of fetishized sex. What seems new to me with Gaultier—and this reflects the sociological fact of a substantial, differentiated and massively prominent homosexual culture—is the fact that fetishized femininity is no longer bound to woman. As queens, fairies and drag queens, men have long since appropriated fetishized femininity for themselves. Gaultier designs the kind of men's fashion in which it is evident that the age of renunciation has been left behind. Men's fashion is no longer made in the name of unmarked sexuality, but is instead unscrupulously marked, covered with all the sex symbols available on the market. Like women, Gaultier's men wear fur coats, bright colors, funky cuts, skin-tight leggings; every form of uniform fetish is indulged. In his Winter 1997 fashion show, one could even catch a glimpse of the codpiece, which I had assumed had definitively run its course. Gaultier deconstructs in his fashion what had still seemed like the most natural thing in the world in the fashion of Yves Saint Laurent or Versace: namely the idea that woman embodies and in this embodiment authenticates fetishized femininity.

On the one hand, man becomes the privileged bearer of fetishized femininity and men's fashion becomes absolutely flamboyant. On the other hand, woman bears the fetish of femininity as a foreign body that is periodically disrupted by masculine appropriation. Particularly appropriate in this respect is Gaultier's response to the Kunigunde-like sex symbols of a Frederick's of Hollywood. While the latter naturalized this fetishized femininity, Gaultier literally turned the process by which a woman can embody the fetishized feminine body inside out. Bustle and bra, garter-belt and corset are worn on top of the dress. Yet another model of this displacement of fetishized femininity can be seen in Vivienne Westwood's 1995 Winter Collection, which was dedicated to the cocotte and her aggressive, exaggerated erotics. Impressive were not only the complicated *décolletés* in corsages that modelled the breasts according to all the tricks of the trade; lifted by the bustle, the *derrière* presented itself charmingly, though in too exaggerated a fashion. This displacement of the feminine drove the Summer Collection *Angels* of Comme des Garçons a step further, to the point that displacement threatened to slip over into disfigurement. Femininity is literally displaced. The bra pads find themselves on the back, the bustle clearly shifted around on to the thigh. This displaced and in its displacement emphasized femininity has a point that is more than just ironic or parodic. The truly novel silhouette oscillates between a misshapen figure reminiscent of the hunchback of Notre Dame, and a completely unexpected and new gracefulness that has definitively abandoned the harmonious symmetry of classical statuary as the measure of Western perfection. Thus with its 1997 Summer Collection Comme des Garçons succeeds in achieving the truly unexpected and unheard of: the creation of a new silhouette out of the displacement of an old and reupholstered femininity. *Like an angel*; not quite of this world?

When Dior or even Saint Laurent dresses women as drag queens, this process is hidden and naturalized. Woman is supposed to be able to embody fetishized femininity perfectly—real to the feel, as it were. Gaultier, however, introduces the traces, the loose ends of drag, into his clothing, and interrupts this process of embodiment by woman, marking so to speak the detour through the masculine body and its distinguishing traits. The most striking example of expropriation and reappropriation in this increasingly vertiginous and meandering circulation of fetishized femininity is the black wool hair trimming the decolleté of a dress in Gaultier's Winter Collection of 1993, which is suggestive of masculine chest hair. And even this hair is doubly encoded and ambiguous. For it can refer just as well to the masculine chest toupée—an essential element of perfected masculinity—as to natural chest hair, which, having been forgotten or overlooked by drag queens, often provides an unintended trim to an otherwise stunningly "feminine" *décolleté*. The most recent manifestation of this dizzying circulation of fetishized femininity seems to be marked by the 1995/1996 Winter Collection, in which man appears as woman as man—a masculine reappropriation of the first feminine appropriation of the dandy fashion.

The point of this matter, of fashion namely as hyper- rather than metafetishism, could be of a Butlerian kind. In a Butlerian argumentation, fashion would have the same function that the homosexual has in relation to the heterosexual couple. It would exhibit social gender as a performative act, in which what it supposedly represents is first produced. Authenticity and realness would not be represented; they would not exist prior to the representation in which they are only allegedly expressed; on the contrary, they would be revealed as products of a performative process. A logic of production would replace a logic of representation. Drag would no longer occupy the rank of a second-class imitation that presupposes a prior, original social gender; rather, it would be subversive to the extent that it mirrored the mimesis at the heart of the dominant gender construction, and thus contested the heterosexual claim to naturalness and authenticity (Butler 1990).

I have attempted to look at the function of hyperfetishism in fashion in a somewhat different light, and thereby to bring both sexual difference and the function of desire into play in a different way. Could one not say that the failure of sexual identity, the representation of gender, is already inscribed within the heterosexual matrix, and precisely for that reason that the reference of the one, feminine, gender to the other, masculine, gender can never be achieved without some remainder? The excess produced by appearance and masquerade cannot represent being, towards which it is directed, without displacement, and this representation must thus for ever remain disfigurement. Would not then the unrestrained fetishization of gender in the name of the feminine be simultaneously the acknowledgment of a failure and of the triumph over this failure? Would not the impossibility of sexual identity, of being entirely man or entirely woman, be both manifest and disguised in fashion as staged fetishism? If the described act of performance can never entirely succeed, but must always go wrong, can sexual identity stage itself in any other way than through a constantly self-undermining enterprise?

Sexual identity would emerge thereby less as a norm or reality than as a phantasm that, in the hypertrophied, unconditional affirmation of the absolute woman and the real man, raises itself up as a dark object of desire—of both heterosexual and homosexual desire. In the blinding appearance (*Schein*) of this dizzying series of stagings, would not the insistence on authenticity and literality finally be revealed as deluded? Euphoric and melancholic aspect of fashion, the terribly beautiful vanity of the world.

Notes

1. This article was translated from the German by Anthony Reynolds.
2. This thesis is undermined by Anne Hollander's *Sex and Suits: A History of Modern Clothing* (1994), in spite of the author's intention. Hollander stresses the classicism of the suit, which is so well made that it seems to be tailored on the model of the Belvedere Apollo, and lends to every man the erotic appeal of a classical hero. That Hollander's panegyric to the masculine suit is as pro-modern as it is anti-fashionable is evident not only where she laments the loss of respect for feminine fashion. The perfection of the masculine suit shows itself for her in the fact that the classicist, with two hundred years of uninterrupted success, stands on the threshold of reaching that eternity of antiquity that is the goal of all classicists.
3. Cf. Karen Ellwanger, "Einkleidungen in 'Weiblichkeit' und 'Männlichkeit' im 19. Jahrhundert," (manuscript).

References

Alewyn, Richard and Karl Salzle. 1959. *Das große Welttheater: Die Epoche der höfischen Feste in Document und Deutung*. Reinbeck bei Hamburg: Rowohlt.

Baudelaire, Charles. 1962. "Éloge du maquillage." In *Le peintre de la vie moderne*. In *Curiosités esthétiques, L'Art romantique et autres œuvres critiques de Baudelaire*, ed. H. Lemaitre. Paris: Classiques Garniers.

Benjamin, Walter. 1983. "Konvolut B 'Mode.'" In *Das Passagen-Werk* I. Frankfurt am Main: Suhrkamp.

Bourdieu, Pierre. 1979. *La distinction: critique sociale du jugement*. Paris: Minuit.

Butler, Judith. 1990. *Gender Trouble: Feminism and the Subversion of Identity*. New York: Routledge.

Ellwanger, Karen. "Einkleidungen in 'Weiblichkeit' und 'Männlichkeit' im 19. Jahrhundert." Manuscript.

Felman, Shoshana. 1981. "Rereading Femininity." *Yale French Studies* 62: 19–44.

Flugel, J. C. 1930. *The Psychology of Clothes*. London: Hogarth Press.

Friedell, Egon. 1931. *Kulturgeschichte der Neuzeit* III. Munich: Beck.

Gottwald, Laura and Janusz Gottwald. 1970. *Frederick's of Hollywood 1947–1973: 26 Years of Mail Order Seduction*. New York: Drake.

Hollander, Anne. 1994. *Sex and Suits: A History of Modern Clothing*. New York: Knopf.

König, René. 1974. *À la Mode: On the Social Psychology of Fashion*, trans. F. Bradley. New York: Seabury Press.

Mentges, Gabriele. 1995. "Der Mensch nach Maß—der vermessene

Mensch." In *Moden und Menschen*. Stuttgart: Design Center Stuttgart.

Musil, Robert. 1978 [1929]. "Die Frau gestern und morgen." *Gesammelte Werke* 8. Reinbeck bei Hamburg: Rowohlt.

Parinaud, André. 1981. *The Unspeakable Confessions of Salvador Dalí*. New York: Morrow.

Simmel, Georg. 1919. "Die Mode." In *Philosophische Kultur*. Leipzig: A. Kroner.

Veblen, Thorstein. 1965[1899]. *The Theory of the Leisure Class: An Economic Study of Institutions*. New York: Viking.

Vinken, Barbara. 1993. *Mode nach der Mode: Geist und Kleid am Ende des Jahrhunderts*. Frankfurt am Main: Suhrkamp.

——. 1995. "Republic, Rhetoric, and Sexual Difference." In *Deconstruction is/in America*, ed. Anselm Haverkamp. New York: New York University Press.

——. 1997. "Eternity—A Frill on the Dress." *Fashion Theory* I: 59–68.

Vischer, Friedrich Theodor. 1879. *Mode und Cynismus*. Stuttgart: K. Wittwer.

von Ihering, Rudolph. 1904(4) [1877]. *Der Zweck im Recht* II. Leipzig: Breithopf & Hartel.

Wolter, Gundula. 1995. "Lieber sterb' ich, als meiner Frau die Hose zu lassen: Zur Kulturgeschichte der Frauenhose." In *Moden und Menschen*. Stuttgart: Design Center Stuttgart.

Zeffirelli, Franco. 1985. *Zeffirelli: An Autobiography*. New York: Weidenfeld and Nicolson.

Fashion Theory, Volume 3, Issue 1, pp.51–80
Reprints available directly from the Publishers.
Photocopying permitted by licence only.
© 1999 Berg. Printed in the United Kingdom.

Veiling Resistance

Fadwa El Guindi

Fadwa El Guindi is Adjunct Full
Professor of Anthropology at
the University of Southern
California. She earned her
Ph.D. in anthropology from the
University of Texas, Austin in
1972 and her BA in political
science from the American
University in Cairo in 1960. Her
most recent book *Veil:
Modesty, Privacy and
Resistance*, is forthcoming
from Berg Publishers.

In the mid-seventies[1] a phenomenon became noticeable in the streets of
Cairo, Egypt that seemed incomprehensible to many observers of the
Egyptian scene and bewildering even to the local people. This was the
strong, visible and growing presence of a new Egyptian woman, with
an appearance unfamiliar to contemporary urban Egypt and to her own
parents. The new woman was a young urban college student completely
"veiled" from head to toe, including the face. Confused at the thought
of a future "veiled" doctor, engineer or pharmacist, many observers
speculated as to the cause of this development. Was this an identity crisis,
our version of America's hippie movement, a fad, youth protest, or
ideological vacuum? An individual psychic disturbance, life-crisis, social
dislocation, or protest against authority?

The Veil Becomes a Movement In Egypt

The contemporary veiling movement passed through several transitional phases after the 1970s, spreading all over the Arab world and among Muslims worldwide (see Wallace 1956 on processual phases in similar movements). Today the Islamic movement continues to grow strong as it enters its third decade. Dress has played a pivotal symbolic, ritual and political role in this dynamic phenomenon. The new vocabulary and dress style embodies a moral/behavioral code. Islam has struggled to position itself *vis-à-vis* the Islamic veil. The response of secularists and Western feminists shows how threatening this trend is to their ideological position. Egypt (with other Arab countries) has accommodated the new movement and put effort into integrating it politically, despite initial attempts by the state to suppress it. Today the veiled and unveiled interact normally in daily life (see Figure 1). Some mothers who originally objected to the veil have adopted it. The Islamic *ziyy* (dress) goes almost unnoticed in Cairo by the local population (see Figure 2).

Figure 1
Youth and middle-aged woman. Note two companion schoolgirls, one with her head covered by the *hijab*, the other with hair uncovered. Photo by F. El Guindi, 1995. Courtesy El Nil Research.

Islamic veiling in Egypt is somewhat different from the situation of the *chador* in Iran. The *chador* is a black head-to-toe wrap that was worn by rural and urban traditional women before the Revolution. The Shah, to Westernize the country, banned it, and the Islamic Revolution, to indigenize tradition, enforced wearing it. In Egypt, the Islamic dress worn after the mid-1970s by women replaced modern secular clothes and is part of a grass-roots activist movement. Unlike Egypt, both Iran and Turkey have long traditions of State-legislated dress reform for both sexes. Although state-discouraged in Egypt, veiling initially met with phenomenal success and spread throughout the urban centers.

Figure 2
Scenes of ordinary daily life in the streets of Cairo, showing how "veiled"
women are integrated with the rest of the people. Photo by F. El Guindi, 1995.
Courtesy El Nil Research.

As some young Egyptian women took up veiling in the mid-1970s, the government increasingly felt the threat of Islamic militancy and looked for solutions. In 1993, the education minister, Husain Kamal Baha' al-Din, sought to combat the spread of Islamic activism by imposing changes in the area of education, such as the transfer or demotion of teachers with activist leanings, a revision of the curriculum, and restrictions on the wearing of the veil (Barraclough 1998:246). However, a ban on wearing the veil at universities was thrown out by the courts. By 1994, attempts to limit the wearing of the veil in schools to students who had their parents' permission were receiving heavy criticism. The minister of education started back-pedaling—conceding that schoolgirls could wear the veil even without parental consent. State interference focusing on the veil remains controversial in Egypt.

In the Ottoman world there were deep roots to the tradition of clothing laws, extending back to the beginning of the empire. And as elsewhere Ottoman clothing laws gave a particular emphasis to head coverings, which typically designated honor and rank. Turbans played a key role in mid-eighteenth century rituals surrounding the Ottoman coronation ceremonies in Istanbul. In the procession, two horsemen each carried turbans of the monarch, tilting them to the right and to the left to receive the homage of the accompanying janissaries. The centrality of the headgear was evident even in the early fourteenth century (Quataert 1997: 403–12).

According to Norton (1997), Turks can judge by appearances and are aware that dress denotes difference, devotion and defiance. "A glance at what a stranger is wearing is often enough to tell them that person's religious and political stance. Clothes can tell them the wearer's defiance of or devotion to the principles of Kemal Ataturk, the reformer who founded the Turkish Republic and banned the fez" (Norton 1997: 149). The present situation in Turkey, like that in most groups in the Islamic world, is such that dress marks the front line in the battle between Islamic advocates and extreme secularists. But whereas the fez was the subject of state legislation, the veil was not, though it was generally discouraged and in some places prohibited. Turkey avoided an outright ban on the veil, the measure the Shah took in Iran, since "forced unveiling of women in Iran [is comparable to] the shock that Westerners would experience if women of all ages were forced to go topless in public" (Goldschmidt 1983; Norton 1997).

In the 1970s there was a one-party effort to create "indigenous dress styles for Muslim women and to legitimize traditional Islamic dress" (Norton 1997: 165). Turkish women began to wear long coats and headscarves. Deep divisions formed between secularists and Muslim advocates (Olson 1985). The word "turban" was introduced in the midst of a headscarf issue. It was ruled that a modern turban may be worn instead of a headscarf. Interestingly, by the mid-1980s in Egypt some of the women who were reluctant at first to wear the *khimar* (a headcovering that covers the hair and extends low to the forehead, comes under the chin to conceal the neck, and falls down over the chest and back) began to wear a turban-like headcovering that had Turkish origins. It was seen as more chic.

Al-Ziyy al-Islami (Islamic Dress)

The Code

Women's Islamic dress, known as *al-ziyy al-Islami*, is an innovative construction that was first worn in the mid-1970s by activists. It does not represent a return to any traditional dress form and has no tangible precedent. There was no industry behind it—not one store in Egypt carried such an outfit. Based on an idealized Islamic vision gradually constructed for the early Islamic community in the seventh century, it was made in the homes by the activists themselves. Privacy, humility, piety and moderation are cornerstones of the Islamic belief system. Luxury and leisure await Muslims in the next world. Some elements of this vision can be supported by reference to the *Qur'an*[2]; others find support in the secondary source of Islamic information, the *Sunna*[3], through the *Hadith*[4]. The 'Prophetic vision' had become idealized through the ages, developing into a model to be emulated via recurring revivalist purifying movements within Islam, just as in the Islamic movement of Egypt in the 1970s.

In the Qur'an (considered the primary and divinely revealed source), but mostly according to the Hadith (a worldly source), evidence suggests that the Prophet Muhammad had paid much attention to a dress code for Muslims in the emerging community, with a specific focus on Muslim men's clothing and bodily modesty during prayer. By comparison, reference to women's body cover is negligible. One such reference, al-Ahzab in *sura* (33:59), distinguishes the status of the Prophet's wives from the rest of the believers, and the other (33:53) protects their privacy from growing intrusions by male visitors.

Men and women in the contemporary Islamic movement who argue for the Islamic dress and behavioral code use as support for their argument two specific *suras* in the Qur'an—al-Nur and al-Ahzab[5]. *Al-Nur*, translates as follows:

> And say to the believing men that they should lower their gaze and guard their genitals [and] say to the believing women that they should lower their gaze and guard their genitals, draw their *khimar* to cover their cleavage [breasts], and not display their beauty, except that which has to appear, except to their husbands, their fathers, their husbands' fathers, their sons, their husbands' sons, their brothers or their brothers' sons, or their sisters' sons, or their women, or the slaves, or eunuchs or children under age;

and they should not strike their feet to draw attention to their hidden beauty. O ye believers turn to God, that ye may attain bliss (Qur'an 24: 30, 31).

Several points can be drawn from this text: (1) the Arabic notions of lowering the gaze and covering the genitals are central to the code; and (2) men are first mentioned as having to abide by these two prescriptions, to control their gaze at women and suppress their passion and forward-ness when interacting with "strange" women. In the Hadith men especially are enjoined to cover their genitals during worship. Unlike other religions, Islam accepts sexuality as a normative aspect of both ordinary and religious life (Mernissi 1975; Marsot 1979; Nelson 1974) and fluidly accommodates both sacred and worldly activity in the same bi-rhythmic space. There is no contradiction between being religious and being sexual. Sex is to be enjoyed in socially approved marriages.

However, outside marriage, behavior between men and women must be desexualized. Both body and interactive space need to be regulated and controlled and both men and women are required to abide by this temporary desexualization to make public interaction between them possible. This presumes that cross-sex interaction would potentially be sexually charged. Islam accepts sexualized, reproductive men and women and guides them to regulate their public behavior.

As the same *sura* (al-Nur) shows, concealing and revealing is very much tied to cultural notions of respectability or the body parts that are considered sexually charged. Islamic mores were being formulated as the *suras* were revealed. The reference to drawing the headveil to cover a woman's cleavage may have been a reaction to the way women in the region prior to birth of the new community seem to have worn clothes that exposed their bodies. Images from what is now modern Yemen, for example, show women from the low-status group of *al-akhdam* (servants) wearing clothing that revealed the breasts. These suggest, not seductive sexuality, but slovenliness.[6] Another prohibition concerns anklets. The phrase "not to strike the feet" is a reference to the practice in which women wore decorative jingling anklets made of heavy metal (silver or gold). It is not the anklet *per se* that is erotic, but the jingling that evokes erotic passions.[7]

Early (1993), in her ethnography on *baladi* (local traditional urban) life in Cairo, describes the traditional *baladi* dress, *milaya laff* (a wrapped black oversheet) draped over a house dress to cover the hair and entire body when in public; the ends of the long wrap are tucked under the arm. From underneath, a tightly knotted scarf covers the hair (p. 70). El-Messiri notes the dimension of sensual playfulness: with high-heeled sandals and tinkling anklets, the dress can combine sexual glamor with modesty (1978: 526, 529).

Within Islam, a woman's sexuality does not diminish her respectability. Islam in fact supports this combined image in womanhood. The Hadith mentions an incident in which the Prophet Muhammad told a woman to color her fingernails with henna so that her hands were not like the hands of men. What Islamic morality forbids is the public flaunting of sexuality. In general, the Islamic code would consider the behavior of the urban *baladi* women in Egypt described in El-Messiri's and Early's ethnographies as exhibitionist. Dressing and moving in a way that draws sexual attention to the body is *tabarruj* (exhibitionist dress and behavior.) It is associated in Islamic perception with Arabian women of *al-Jahiliyya* (the Days of Ignorance or pre-Islamic days) and was frowned upon during the formative years of the Islamic community in the seventh century.

The Dress

In the contemporary revival, the dress code was translated this way: men and women wear full-length *gallabiyyas* (*jilbab* in standard Arabic), loose-fitting to conceal body contours, in solid austere colors made out of opaque fabric. They lower their gaze in cross-sex public interaction and refrain from body or dress decoration or colors that draw attention to their bodies. The dress code for men consists of sandals, baggy trousers with loose-top shirts in off-white, or alternatively (and preferably) a long loose white *gallabiyya*. They grow a *lihya* (a full beard trimmed short), with an optional mustache. Hair is to be kept shoulder-length. This last feature has not been sustained, and was eventually dropped. The general behavioral code of austerity and restraint has support in Qur'anic segments that repeatedly stress the undesirability of arrogance and an exhibitionist demeanor.[8]

Figure 3
One *muhajjaba* [head-covered woman] and one *munaqqaba* [face-covered woman] as they cross paths on a street in Cairo on an ordinary day. Photo by F. El Guindi, 1995. Courtesy El Nil Research.

Similarly, women wear the *hijab* which consists of *al-jilbab* (ankle-length, long-sleeved, loose-fitted dress) and *al-khimar*, a headcovering that covers the hair and extends low to the forehead, comes under the chin to conceal the neck, and falls down over the chest and back. The common colors used by women during the first decade of the movement were beige, brown, navy, deep wine, white and black (see Figure 3). This dress is worn while engaging fully in daily affairs in public social space in which not only their gender is accepted but also their sexual identity. Austere dress form and behavior therefore are not accompanied by withdrawal, seclusion, or segregation.

The voluntary informal dress code extends beyond clothing to a general demeanor characterized by serious behavior and an austere manner, an ideal applied to both sexes. Some women more conservatively add *al-niqab*, which covers the entire face except for the eye slits; at the most extreme, a woman would also wear gloves and opaque socks to cover her hands and feet. This trend has been spreading throughout the Arab world, particularly among university students. Chatty describes a similar trend occurring in south-eastern Arabia (Chatty 1997).

During the first decade of the movement in Egypt the dress code for women corresponded to the degree of Islamic knowledgeability and reading, as well as to a step on a scale of leadership among women. The more intensely covered the college woman, the more "serious" her public behavior, and the more knowledgeable she is in Islamic sources, the higher she was on the scale of activist leadership among women. She would lead discussions, for example, in mosques and in women students' lounges between lectures. This correspondence dissolved as the movement spread outside the university campuses and as the *hijab* became part of normal life and was integrated with secular life in Cairo and the other major cities.

This Islamic dress was introduced by college women in the movement and was not imposed by the al-Azhar authorities, who ordinarily prescribe Islamic behavior by issuing decrees. Instead, this was a bottom-up movement. By dressing this way in public these young women conveyed their vision of Islamic ideals by becoming exemplary contemporary models. Encoded in the dress style is an affirmation of an Islamic identity and morality and a rejection of Western materialism, consumerism, commercialism, and values. The vision behind the Islamic dress is rooted in these women's understanding of early Islam and, as earlier presented, in primary and secondary textual sources. But it is a contemporary movement about contemporary issues.

Clearly, the movement is not simply about a dress code. Like early Islam in Madina, this activism espouses egalitarianism, community, identity, privacy, and justice. It condemns exhibitionism in dress and behavior, which was characteristic of *al-jahiliyya* (the pre-Islamic era). Hence, al-Jahiliyya is not just a historical moment, but a state and a condition of society that can recur at any time. Reserve and restraint in behavior, voice and body movement are not restrictions—they symbolize a renewal of traditional cultural identity.

Veiling in Two Feminisms

The Egyptian feminist movement at the turn of the century was described as a secular movement that "brought together Muslim and Christian women of the upper and middle classes[9] who identified [themselves] as Egyptians" (Badran 1995b: 45). Leila Ahmed does not see it in such monolithic terms. In a discussion linking Western colonialism and feminism, Ahmed distinguishes two strands of feminism propounded by Egypt's "First Feminists" (1992:169–188). There is the Westward-looking feminism espoused by Huda Sha'rawi (1879–1947)[10] and another, advocated by Malak Hifni Nasif (1886–1918)[11] that did not affiliate itself with Westernization.

Groundedness of feminists in their own culture has been largely overlooked in the discourse on feminism.[12] Fundamental to a genuine Arabo-Islamic society are mastery of the Arabic language (formal not colloquial) and access to Islamic knowledge. These two cornerstones of the culture had gradually become the domains of men—a masculinization process that distanced many women from the core of their culture. This process is connected to the valuation for "foreign" languages (at the expense of the Arabic language) that has developed among the urbanized ascribed aristocracy and spread among urban achieved-status groups. Speaking "soft" Arabic with French loan words became feminine and chic. A corollary practice was the informal adoption of a husband's last name in lieu of one's maiden name. It should be noted in this regard that Arab women have financial autonomy. The legal system requires that a woman should keep her maiden name after marriage. Officially, the state in Arab society does not recognize a husband's name even when it is informally adopted by women. Nasif, true to her views and her self-image, continued to use her natal family name after marriage, whereas Huda first simplified her name from Nur al-Huda (her name at birth) to Huda, and then upon marriage changed her last name from Sultan (her father's name) to Sha'rawi (her husband's name)—a social (not an official or a legal) practice borrowed by urbanized women to validate their modern, feminine, and chic image.

A superficial familiarity with Islamic knowledge acquired casually through male relatives also became the norm among women. One can only speculate about the factors that led to this state of affairs. Women identified with French culture at the expense of Arabic, which was considered *déclassé*. Lacking the necessary command of the Arabic language, Huda Sha'rawi, the pioneer feminist of the Arab world, did not write her own memoirs. Instead she dictated a chronicle of events to her male secretary, who had a command of the Arabic language.

Despite her prominence as a feminist leader, she was distanced from her native language, and therefore not a complete insider in her own culture. Instead, she mastered foreign languages. "She was educated at home by tutors in both Turkish and French, the languages of a lady of the time" (Fernea and Bezirgan 1977: 193). One must note that those "ladies" (see Marsot 1978) made up an insignificant percentage of the Egyptian population, and their programs were mostly relevant within their own circles. While Huda was tutored in foreign languages her brother was receiving private Arabic lessons.[13]

This had not always been the case in Egypt. Al-Sayyid Marsot mentions that in the eighteenth century the greater masses of both sexes were illiterate, but "among the elites both men and women were literate in religion and in language [and] the *ulama* (male religious scholars) and *alimat* (female religious scholars) were more educated than any other sector of society" (1995: 14,15). Colonial and missionary pressures at the turn of the century as well as consumerist and secularizing trends in the twentieth century led women away from rights they already had in Islam—most importantly the right (with precedents in Islam) to full participation in the Islamic process, teaching, and worship. By submitting to these distancing trends, women excluded themselves from the two most relevant spheres (the Arabic language and Islamic studies) that most crucially regulate and sanction their lives, engender dignity and respect, and legitimize their rights and privileges. These became dominated by men.

As early as the 1870s and 1880s, before Egyptian organized feminism developed, Egyptian women were publishing their writings and were engaged in public speaking. They wrote poetry, prose, biographies, articles, and essays and published them in the mainstream press at a time when publishing was new to Egypt. By the 1890s an emergent "sisterhood" of exchanges of letters and circulation of books expanded and took new forms. Badran describes the environment of the turn of the century in Egypt as "an urban harem culture, the site of the first emergence of women's feminist awareness and nascent feminist expression" (Badran 1995a: 4). Collective debate grew through "salons" held by the women of the aristocracy and expanded with the founding by non-aristocratic women of a women's press.

Egyptian women, Muslim and Christian, were positioning their liberation *vis-à-vis* the simultaneously rising nationalism that grew up in response to colonial intervention.[14] Colonial domination was complete and humiliating, particularly in its very denial of Egyptianness. The British colonizers referred to Egyptians as "natives" or the "native race." Their avoidance of the term "Egyptian" made Egyptians seem nameless and nationless. It was in this climate that both nationalism and feminism took hold. Egyptianness and women's rights rose simultaneously. Paradoxically, the degree of political or personal affiliation with the colonizer became a barometer of commitment to nationalist activism.

It is significant in this regard that, according to Badran, Huda Sha'rawi's father, Sultan Pasha, was implicated in assisting British intervention in Egypt (1995a: 11).[15]

Women had already begun to debate their position on these issues when men, in search of factors behind the demise of their country, began questioning existing social practices with regard to gender and formulated what many considered to be feminist positions in the process. These men were highly educated, had legal training, and had been exposed to European thought. Consequently, a men's discourse on women's issues (questionably characterized as feminist) emerged in the Arab world (Badran 1995a: 13–16). Unlike women's organized feminism, the veil was central to men's "feminist" discourse. Women were drawn into the debate and popular periodicals became partisan publications. Three periodicals[16] were "staunch defenders of the veil [and two][17] condemned the veil . . . Muslims, Jews, and Christians all wrestled with the question of veiling" (Baron 1989: 372, 379).

A prominent Egyptian man who provoked heated controversy and debate was Qasim Amin, who came to be regarded by many as the founder of feminism in Arab culture. The response to his book *Tahrir Al-Mar'a* (The Liberation of Woman), published in 1899, was intense, and opposition to its message was vociferous. In the book, he advocated primary school education for women and reform of the laws on polygyny and divorce. Were these considered radical proposals at the time? Ahmed notes that they were not new. These issues had been proposed in the 1870s and 1880s, perhaps even earlier, by Muslim intellectuals who had argued for women's education and called for reforms in matters of polygyny and divorce "without provoking violent controversy" (1992: 145). By the 1890s the issue of educating women beyond the primary level was uncontroversial and girls' schools were established. So why was there such a strong reaction to Amin's work?

A closer look reveals that Amin called, not for feminist reforms, but rather for a fundamental social and cultural change for Egypt and other Muslim countries, a Europeanization of Arab culture as it were, in which women's issues were embedded. Central to this reform, proposed as the key to change and progress in society, was the call for abolishing the veil.

Tal'at Harb, a wealthy Egyptian industrialist entrepreneur who pioneered modern banking in Egypt, responded strongly to Amin. He is described as having "defended and upheld Islamic practices" (Ahmed 1992: 164). But in fact Harb used Islamic language and selected quotations from Christian and Muslim scriptures and Western and Muslim men of learning to defend and uphold a perspective that is not much different from Amin's Western vision of female domesticity: that the wife's duty was to attend to the physical, mental, and moral needs of her husband and children (Harb 1905 [1899]: 21). First, these are the same duties ascribed to her by Amin. To modernize Muslim society Amin wanted to abandon its "backward" ways and follow the Western path, which of course required changing women. His call for women's education was based on the idea that women needed education in order to manage the household, a responsibility that entails many skills. "It is the wife's responsibility to establish the family budget . . . to manage servants . . . to make her home attractive and appealing to her husband, to enjoy food, drink and sleep, and not seek comfort elsewhere, with neighbors or in public places. But her first and most important duty is to raise and socialize the children, physically, mentally, and morally" (Amin 1916, Vol. 2: 31, my translation). Borrowing from Western notions of domesticity and womanhood in order to validate what is characteristically an Arab quality of family relations, Amin wrote that the adult man is nothing but what his mother made him to be from childhood. "*The essence of this book and the message I wish to impart to all men . . . is the special relationship between a man and his mother . . . it is impossible to produce successful men without mothers capable of enabling them to be successful.* This is the noble duty that advanced civilization has given to woman in our age and which she fulfills in advanced societies" (1976, Vol. 2: 78–79; translation mine, emphasis in original)[18]. Most significantly, Amin reaffirmed the special and unique mother-son relationship already inherent in Arab society by using European notions of female domesticity.

Second, it is questionable whether Tal'at Harb's views would be characterized as Islamic. Qasim Amin, on the other hand, was explicitly positioned outside the Islamic spectrum. He was a French-educated lawyer whose rationale in calling for change in the position of women and for abolishing the veil was not much different from the colonial/ missionary agenda. The ideas espoused by the British colonial official Lord Cromer, who embodied the colonizer's posture and agenda, and the missionaries, whose strategy was to undermine Islam and Arab tradition, were reflected in Amin's book. Amin's text also assumed and declared the inherent superiority of Western civilization and the inherent backwardness of Muslim societies: he wrote that anyone familiar with "the East" had observed "the backwardness of Muslims . . . wherever they are." Among Muslims he saw a hierarchy that put the Egyptians at the bottom[19]—Muslim civilization in general is represented as semicivilized compared to that of the West. As Ahmed put it: "In the course of making his argument, Amin managed to express . . . a generalized contempt for Muslims . . . often in lavishly abusive detail" (Ahmed 1992: 156). Veiling was not a practice confined to Muslims; it was an urban phenomenon associated mostly with the upper classes. The Coptic intellectual Salama Musa noted in his memoirs that his mother and two married sisters wore the long veil until about 1907 or 1908, and that it was through missionary influence that Christian women began to drop the practice. Also Qasim Amin's wife continued to wear the veil. He tried to enforce unveiling on his daughters despite efforts to the contrary from his own uncle.[20]

Both Amin and Harb claimed to be concerned with women's liberation. They differed in their frameworks but reached similar conclusions. One exception is the veil. Harb's women must veil, and Amin's must unveil. The argument between Harb and Amin was not, as it is commonly characterized, feminist versus antifeminist,[21] but rather reflected two muddled versions of domesticity, a Western female domesticity versus an indigenous man's vision of female domesticity. Islam was not in any serious way the ideological basis for either position.[22] Contradictions abound in both. In appropriating a women's issue, men polarized discourse surrounding the veil.

Amin's book, then, can be seen as fueling feminist debate rather than simply pioneering feminist reform in Egypt. It put on center stage the colonial narrative of women, in which the veil and the treatment of women epitomized Islamic inferiority, and entered the colonial agenda of appropriation of resources and culture into mainstream Arabic discourse and programs of reform. The opposition it generated similarly marks "the emergence of an Arabic narrative developed in resistance to the colonial narrative. This narrative of resistance appropriated, in order to negate them, the symbolic terms of the originating narrative" (Ahmed 1992:164).

By 1910 sensitivity toward the nuances of veiling and unveiling was established. The newspaper *al-'Afaf* began publication in Cairo in 1910 "proclaiming itself the mouthpiece of women" (Baron 1989: 370). In the twenty-sixth issue of its first volume it used as a frontispiece a drawing of a woman standing in front of the pyramids and the sphinx, holding her arm aloft with a banner that read "modesty is my motto." Across her face she wore a light, translucent veil. The mouth and nose were revealed through the transparent fabric and the eyes were not covered. Baron (1989: 28) notes that the paper was criticized (see *al-'Afaf* 1911: 1)[23] and that three issues later the image was revised. The redrawn veil was thick and nontransparent, and the nose, face and chin were not revealed through it. Revealed, however, are the complex subtleties entailed in the reaction to this visual imagery of the veil and womanhood.

Interestingly, removing the veil was not part of the official feminist agenda at the time. According to Badran (1995a), unveiling, which had been of concern only to urban women, "had never been part of the EFU's (Egyptian Feminist Union) formal agenda" (pp. 94–96). The phrase used in the discourse surrounding the context of lifting the "veil" was *raf' al-higab* (the lifting of the *hijab*). Ironically, what secular feminists lifted was the traditional face veil (*burqu'*), which is rooted in cultural tradition and history rather than in Islamic sources, not the *hijab*. In her speech at the Feminist conference in Rome, Sha'rawi specified the face veil (*burqu'* or *yashmik*), not *hijab*, as a barrier to women's advancement (253, 254; see Kahf 1998). When Huda Sha'rawi dramatically cast off the veil in 1923, it was the face veil she removed, not the *hijab*. Further, the act mirrored a change already taking place, as the debate over the issue of veiling and unveiling shows.

It is not trivial that Huda Sha'rawi only removed the face cover (*burqu'* or *yashmik*) but kept the head covering. Technically, therefore, Sha'rawi never "lifted the *hijab*." Some attribute her success in feminist nationalist leadership, compared to Doria Shafiq (1914–1976),[24] for example, to the fact that she respected this tradition. In her *Memoirs* there is a segment in which she mentions being congratulated for "my success in arriving at lifting the *hijab* . . . but wearing the *hijab shar'i*" (lawful *hijab*—used specifically to mean the Islamic *hijab*) (Sha'rawi 1981: 291). The distinction made is important, and becomes central to the debate on contemporary veiling. Sha'rawi lifted the traditional customary veil and wore the *hijab* in the manner that finds support in Islamic sources.[25] Significantly, she was decorated with the state's highest honor, *Nishan al-Kamal* (Medal of Perfection). Badran (1995a) describes how in the first two decades of the twentieth century feminist women like Huda Sha'rawi and Malak Hifni Nasif (Bahithat al-Badiya) retained the veil, because "uncovering the face was premature [and] society was not ready for it" (Badran 1995a: 22, 23).

Of the early feminists, Nabawiyya Musa, the first college graduate and the one who was not from the aristocracy, removed her face covering unceremonially around 1909. "Bahithat al-Badiya died in 1918 without having unveiled" (Badran 1995a: 23). The comment by Nasif that after social change "I would approve of unveiling *for those who want it*" (Nasif 1962: 275–279, emphasis added) confirms, contrary to falsely publicized claims, the tolerant stance of early twentieth-century Egyptian feminism with regard to veiling. It also brings out an element in Nasif's feminism absent in other programs—choice on the part of women.

Huda Sha'rawi unveiled ceremonially in a public political feminist act in 1923 upon returning from a feminist meeting in Rome—an act of far-reaching symbolic significance.[26] Its impact and ripple effect was felt beyond her narrow circle of the elite.[27] The gesture has entered the lore on women's liberation and, as lore, is alive and is continually embellished. Evidence in photographs and reports reveals how girls had begun to appear unveiled in schools,[28] in the streets,[29] and in protests between 1910 and 1919 (Baron 1989:379). It has been observed that in Cairo before the First World War Egyptian women were far more advanced than their Lebanese counterparts. Egyptian women, it was observed by a Lebanese writer, are "more emancipated than us . . . they saw the world with unveiled eyes [unlike our women] who did not see the world except from behind black veils" (Khalidi 1978: 64). So unveiling was already publicly visible before 1914. While Sha'rawi's dramatic gesture did not mark the beginning of unveiling, her social and political position in society gave the process celebrity and legitimacy.

The *hijab* worn by Muslim and Christian women at the turn of the century is different in meaning from the *hijab* worn by college women in the 1970s. The first was characterized as "a national Egyptian dress for upper-class women, then called *al-habara*" (Nabarawi 1979).[30] It consisted of a full-length skirt, a head cover, and *al-burqu'* (a face covering from below the eyes down to the chest) and was worn by Muslim and Christian women. In her memoirs, Huda Sha'rawi used the term *izari* (my cloak) in referring to what she commonly wore as a wrap when she went out. She did not seem to use the term *hijab* except in the context of the political act of lifting the veil (Sha'rawi 1981: 89).[31] Ahmed notes that Amin's book, the debate it generated, and the issues of class and tradition with which the debate became inscribed, may be regarded as the precursor and prototype of the debate around the veil (Ahmed 1992: 164). This is not quite so, however, since by the time Amin published his work in 1899 the debate had already begun in the press.

Reacting to the writings of European-influenced Egyptian men who advocated the lifting of the veil for women, Malak Hifni Nasif saw a nuanced "male domination enacted through [their] discourse of the veil" (Ahmed 1992: 179). She opposed mandatory unveiling. Badran does not distinguish between the feminism of Nasif and that of Sha'rawi. She sees the latter as a continuation of the same struggle. After Nasif's death at a young age "Sha'rawi publicly pledged to continue her struggle on behalf of women" (Badran 1995c: 230). But Ahmed does.

The two leading women espoused two feminist views: one more authentically Egyptian, the other Western-influenced. This different-iation is important because research increasingly shows that feminism is rooted in culture. It challenges Western feminism's claims of univers-ality, which dominate discourse and research in the West. Differences exist among feminisms and multiple feminist strands can exist within the same society. Background, upbringing, education, social class and political ideology all influence the content of feminism and feminist goals. And just as Western feminism is solidly rooted in European and American cultures, the Egyptian feminism of Western-influenced Egyptians can be different from a feminism that is more deeply and authentically rooted in the culture and tradition of Egypt, despite apparent similarities.

The Arabic language and Islamic knowledge mattered to Malak Hifni Nasif, but were not included in the official feminist agenda as it developed under the leadership of Huda Sha'rawi, which stressed women's suffrage, education reform, health services, and employment opportunities. Nasif, in contrast with Huda Sha'rawi,[32] was highly proficient in the Arabic language. She gave lectures in fluent Arabic and was a prolific Arabic writer. She was comfortable with her roots and well grounded in her native (Arabic) language and Arab culture.

In her *Memoirs* Sha'rawi recounts how the Egyptian delegation to the International Women's conference in Rome in 1923 vowed "that we would follow in the footsteps of the women in Europe in the awakening of our women so that we could take our land to its rightful place among the advanced nations"[33] (1981: 252). The same frame of reference is used in the language of the agenda submitted by the Sha'rawi-led Egyptian Feminist Union to the government. The rationale for the feminist program was couched neither in terms of absolute feminism and women's entitlement, nor in terms espousing the preservation of tradition. Rather, the rationale was in order for Egypt "to reach a level of glory and might like that reached by the civilized nations" (1981: 262).

Looking up to Europeanization of behavior and culture was made integral to the inscripted culture of the aristocracy. Internalizing a valorization of European culture while undermining native culture, its members presented a "gallicized" public social self. That was the way to convey and validate their class. However, the implication of this colonization of selves and minds is an area of research that has not received sufficient attention.

The principal beneficiaries of the British reform measures and the increased involvement in European capitalism were the European residents of Egypt, the Egyptian upper classes, and the new middle class of rural notables and men educated in Western-type secular schools who became the civil servants and the new intellectual elite. Whether trained in the West or in the Western-type institutions established in Egypt, these "modern" men with their new knowledge challenged the traditionally and religiously trained *ulama* (the al-Azhar authoritative scholars of Islam), displacing them as administrators, bureaucrats and educators to become transmitters of the newly valued secular scholarship and secular approach to society. Traditional knowledge itself became devalued as outmoded and backward. The resulting proposals seemed to have adopted the weaknesses in both cultures, the colonizing and the colonized.

Nasif's agenda stressed two significant elements absent in Sha'rawi's feminist agenda. First, she demanded that all fields of higher education be opened to women. Information on the specific fields that were reserved for men is significant here. In the West the fields that were "open" for women were mostly the "soft" fields of art and home economics. American women until recently did not tend to go into the professional schools of medicine and engineering or majors such as mathematics or economics. In the Arab world, studies of patterns in higher education (El Guindi 1985, 1986) show that, when higher education became widely accessible in the 1950s, enrollments were balanced between the sexes. The distribution in "soft" fields and professional majors was similar for both sexes. Yet while women were significantly present in medicine and engineering (valued for modern society), they were absent in two particular majors: Arabic Studies and Islamic Studies. This is where cultural context is important in determining which obstacles facing women are relevant for their liberation.

When Nasif demanded that *all* fields be made open to women, was she concerned about Arabic and Islamic Studies? This very issue would become relevant several decades later in the 1970s.

Second, she demanded that space be made in mosques for women to participate in public prayer. By demanding that mosques be made accessible to women, Nasif had established an agenda that recognizes what is core in the culture (see Nasif 1909). Her agenda was Islamic, her goals feminist. These premises presupposed a strong populist movement that is Islamic feminist.

Clearly, whereas Sha'rawi was socialized into a world that attached high value to French culture above local tradition, Nasif was firmly rooted in Arabo-Islamic culture. But one cannot easily characterize Nasif as a traditionalist. In their ultimate goal of advancing women's rights, Nasif and Sha'rawi did not differ. Had Nasif lived longer, however, it is very likely that two parallel (organized) feminisms would have developed—one grounded in Arabo-Islamic culture, the other in European culture and feminism.

The discourse of colonialism incorporated a language of feminism and used the issue of women's position in Islamic societies as the focus of attack on those societies. Men serving the colonial administration, such as Cromer in Egypt,[34] who ironically opposed feminism in his own country, England, espoused in the colonial context a rhetoric of feminism that attacked Egyptian men for upholding practices that degraded their women. This posture of subversion and appropriation of the colonized culture can be interpreted as the colonizing power's attempt to legitimize its own domination and justify its occupation policies. The kind of feminism emerging out of this colonial context becomes an alternative form of dominance that gives its men and women a sense of superiority. By adopting it, Egyptian men accepted and Egyptian women reproduced their own subordination within their culture as well as their country's subordination to European dominance.

Two Notions of Gender

In the course of my analysis of Islamic activism (El Guindi 1998) two conceptions of gender emerge. The first individuates society,[35] secularizes culture, and feminizes social, political, and moral issues. Its agenda prioritizes women's problems, mostly independent of cultural constructions, and often segregated from society as a whole and from political affairs. While it assumes universality, this notion originates in Western thought and is embedded in cultural values constructed out of a Euro-Christian ethos, relations of domination, and the colonial encounter. It is based on constructs of polarities. Filtered through lenses of Christo-European constructions, efforts to understand the Middle East have resulted in distorted perspectives about Islamic constructions of gender, space and sexuality. For example, gender roles are described as domestic (private) versus public—a division that better describes Western European society but distorts understanding of Arab and Islamic society. Also, piety is mistakenly separated from worldliness and sexuality, leading to the ingrained focus on seclusion and virginity and thus missing nuances characteristic of Islamic space and privacy as they pertain to veiling. Looking at Islamic culture through these lenses of distortion reveals violations of ideal separations between the worldly and the religious, between Church and State, between domestic and public.

Instead of the polarity that characterizes Western constructions, Islamic principles insist on the integration of dualities. Hence we encounter a modality of polarity (Western) versus a modality of relational integration (Arabo-Islamic).

It is within the latter model that we locate the second conception of gender, which is embedded within cultural tradition and Islamic activism and is contextualized in local, regional and cultural history. This conception is more relevant to an objective understanding of Muslim women's activism. Approaching Muslim women's rights through liberal feminist agendas cannot be effective because these agendas are based on the Western experience and derive from Western values; hence they are irrelevant to most issues of concern to Muslim women. Matters pertaining to women and the family are based on scripturalist-derived decrees and laws. To be effective, these issues must be dealt with within the same framework that created them. Feminism within the context of Islam can provide the only path to empowerment and liberation that avoids challenging the whole of the culture (Mir-Hosseini 1996).

But there is another point. Reaffirmation of traditional values and identities also feeds from the same Arabo-Islamic source. One can choose either the liberal feminist or the Islamic feminist path, but in neither can reform be effected or goals be achieved without direct access to primary Islamic knowledge in Arabic. This point had not escaped Doria Shafiq, who struggled to find legitimacy for her feminism even among feminists. She recognized the need to master Islamic knowledge and to communicate in the Arabic language. Any Europeanized activities were considered marginal (see the ethno-biography of Doria Shafik by Nelson (1996)).

The Egyptian college women who pioneered the Islamic movement in the 1970s penetrated precisely these culturally relevant realms. They were reading primary sources, although much of their energy was spent in justifying their newly constructed dress and defending their posture *vis-à-vis* society. Their dress gradually became a uniform and a model for public demeanor and cross-sex relations. Mainstream society and Islam began to accommodate them. Increasingly, Egyptians dressed more conservatively. Islamic dress was mass-produced and made available at a low cost. Commercial stores specialized in its sale, thereby making it chic and appealing, and hairdressers opened special sections for the *muhaggabat* (see Figure 4).

Figure 4
Hairdresser in Cairo with sign:
"For Women, For *Muhajjabat*.
A special section—Manicure,
Pedicure." Photo by F. El
Guindi, 1995. Courtesy El Nil
Research.

Islamic Feminism

Another feminism, which I label Islamic feminism,[36] set itself unambiguously apart from the two feminisms of Nasif and Sha'rawi when the prominent pioneer, Zaynab al-Ghazali, carved an alternative path. Al-Ghazali was born in 1917, the daughter of an al-Azhar-educated independent religious teacher and cotton merchant. She was privately tutored in Islamic studies in the home, and afterwards attended a public secondary school. Her father encouraged her to become an Islamic leader. She obtained certificates in Hadith and Tafsir.

Al-Ghazali had first begun her activist career by participating in the activities of the secular feminist organization founded by Huda Sha'rawi, who was her mentor, as she was to many prominent women. After joining the Egyptian Feminist Union she became dissatisfied and sought another path for women's rights—one from within Islam. Rejecting the Western woman as a model for Muslim women, Zaynab al-Ghazali abandoned the secular Egyptian Feminist Union and founded, at the age of eighteen, Jama'at al-Sayyidat al-Muslimat (the Muslim Women's Association), which was active from 1936 to 1964.[37] She published and gave weekly lectures to thousands of women at the Ibn Tolon Mosque (Hoffman-Ladd 1995: 64–66). "The Association published a magazine, maintained an orphanage, offered assistance to poor families, and mediated family disputes" (1995: 64). Her public activism and mastery of and leadership in Islamic issues set her apart, and qualified her to lead women within the Islamic fold.

An autonomous, strong-minded woman who was dedicated to learning Islam from childhood and gained credentials that qualified her to teach it, she divorced her first husband who allegedly interfered with her Islamic activities. She espoused Islamic ideals that supported family values while she also developed into a prominent activist leader in Islamic teaching and organizing (Hoffman-Ladd 1995; Hoffman 1985). Neither she nor the Islamic leadership of the Muslim Brotherhood saw her combined roles as contradictory.

When al-Ghazali first joined the Association of Huda Sha'rawi she had established her commitment to women's rights and to serving women's interests. When she switched from the secularist feminist path to the path of Islam to reach these goals, she revealed her own conviction of Islam and awareness of its importance in ordinary people's lives. The movement's success and wide appeal legitimized Islam as potentially liberating for women. When Hassan al-Banna, founder of the Muslim Brotherhood,[38] sought her cooperation and suggested that both associations work together to unify the movement, she insisted on keeping her organization autonomous. Her leadership was not questioned by men or women in the general movement. However, she obviously posed a threat to the state—sufficiently so that she was arrested, imprisoned, and reportedly tortured. She describes her experience in her prison memoirs (al-Ghazali 1977).

The seeds of Islamic feminism were sown long before al-Ghazali formed the organization for Muslim women in 1936. In 1908 some Muslim women in Egypt led by Fatima Rashid, wife of Muhammad Farid Wajdi, owner of the nationalist newspaper *al-Dustur* (The Constitution) formed an organization, *Tarqiyat al-Mar'a* (Refinement of the Woman), through which Rashid urged women to adhere to religion and veiling as "the symbol of our Muslim grandmothers" (Rashid 1908a: 76; 1908b: 84). Modesty, morality and Islamic principles (i.e., the view that Islamic law gives advantages to women) were its founding principles. The newspaper *al-'Afaf* endorsed this affirmation of culture and religion against foreign intervention and customs (Baron 1989: 380).

The movement led by Zaynab al-Ghazali was modeled after the other contemporaneous organized feminist groups and, like them, it was characterized by having a charismatic female leader at the helm. There was a large difference in the size of the organizations' memberships. Records show that membership in the Islamic organization was exponentially larger than in Huda Sha'rawi's. Smaller still was that of Doria Shafik, who was seen as an extremist secularist Europeanized feminist. Her core supporters were from Europe or were family and friends.

The movement that emerged in the 1970s is different. Above all, it is populist. It is also grounded in culture and in Islam, and never had any formal organization or membership. It erupted everywhere in the main urban centers of Egypt, particularly in the universities, ultimately spreading outward. It was a grass-roots, voluntary youth movement, possibly begun by women, which mixed backgrounds, lifestyles and social boundaries. Its impact was powerful. Out of it emerged a grass-roots Islamic feminism (El Guindi 1982a, 1982b, 1983, 1992, 1996, 1997).

This thread of Islamic feminism is left out of chronicles of Egyptian feminism. Secularist-bound scholars either deny its existence or ideologically dismiss any scholarly discussion of such formulations (even empirical studies) as apology.[39] Nevertheless, it is feminist because it seeks to liberate womanhood; it is Islamic because its premises are embedded in Islamic principles and values. Yet, in some senses, the liberal Western-influenced feminism of the aristocracy and the Islamic one are not far apart. Both are about emancipation of women. The early feminist lifting of the face veil was about emancipation from exclusion; the voluntary wearing of the *hijab* since the mid-seventies is about liberation from imposed, imported identities, consumerist behaviors, and an increasingly materialist culture. Further, a principal aim has been to allow women greater access to Islamic literacy.

In the 1980s the movement shifted from establishing an Islamic identity and morality to asserting Islamic nationalism, engaging in participatory politics, and resisting local authoritarian regimes, colonial occupation and Western dominance. Embedded in today's *hijab* is imagery that combines notions of respectability, morality, identity, and resistance. Women (and men) who oppose the *hijab* are opposing the absence of choice, as in Iran, Turkey, Algeria, and Palestine. Resistance through *the hijab* or against it, in tangible form as attire or in intangible form as a code of behavior, has generated a dynamic discourse around gender, Islamic ideals, Arab society, and women's status and liberation.

Notes

1. Fieldwork for data on which this article is partially based was conducted in Egypt on many research trips (1976, 1979, 1980, 1981–2), and annual research trips from 1984 until 1997). Support was provided by a faculty grant from UCLA African Studies Center (1976), a Ford Foundation grant No. 770-0651 (1979, 1980) (as part of the UCLA Interdisciplinary Ford Foundation project, *Rich and Poor States in the Middle East*, directed by the late Malcolm Kerr under the auspices of the Center for Near Eastern Studies), and a Fulbright Fellowship (Islamic Civilization Senior Research Scholarship) grant No. 80-006-IC (1981–2). Subsequent trips were funded by El Nil Research, Los Angeles.

   The author acknowledges with gratitude support from El Nil Research in granting permission to use the ethnographic photos from its archives selected for use in this article. This article is a shortened version of a chapter to appear in the forthcoming book being published by Berg Publishers: *Veil: Modesty, Privacy and Resistance*.

2. The word *Qur'an*, derives from words that mean both "recite" and "read." It is based on the oral revelations transmitted to God's messenger, Muhammad, which were recorded upon his request on any available material: cloth, leather, bone, stone, etc. These were meticulously compiled and written up. The *Qur'an* is divided into Suras, and the Suras into Ayahs.

3. The *Sunna*, which means "the path," with reference to the path of the Prophet, consists of actions, sayings, and deeds of the Prophet Muhammad as transmitted by reliable sources close to him.

4. The compilation of the *Sunna*, which occurred long after the death of the Prophet, was a scholarly process carried out by Imams; its results were published in written form. The written books containing the *Sunna* are called *Hadith*, a word that translates as "Prophetic Narratives." There are nine recognized Hadith Compendia. Each is divided into books by subject, and chapters by constituent topics.

5. They are most certainly not suggestive of the eroticism of women's breasts (as in American culture), as there is no ethnographic evidence to that effect. Breasts are traditionally more associated with maternity than with sex, as is the case in many cultures outside the Euro-American fold. The sexualization of breasts is a Western influence.

6. Another part of a Middle Eastern woman's body that is considered erotic is her eyes.

7. *Sura* 4: 36; 17: 37; 28: 83; 31: 18; 40: 75; 57: 23.

8. The classist characterization of Egypt using the tripartite classification of lower, middle, and upper that is used in most writings on Egypt is too simple and too ethnocentric to be of value in understanding the groupings in modern urban and traditional urban quarters, and rural Egypt. Wealth, education, religion, etc. do not lend themselves to neat "class" membership. There are very wealthy butchers proud of the *Baladi* identity and living in traditional urban quarters, for example. There are educated, Westernized, urbanized individuals with strong rural backgrounds who visit their relatives in the villages. For the purposes of discussion of urban movements and class organization prior to the Revolution of the 1950s, which is the point where one can (though still simplistically) talk about an emergent middle class, it is best to use the dichotomy that has gone out of use: ascribed-status class and achieved-status class. This would be particularly useful in discussions on the Western-influenced feminist movement.

9. Huda Sha'rawi was born Nur al-Huda Sultan in 1897 in Minya in southern Egypt, the daughter of Sultan Pasha, a wealthy landowner, and Iqbal Hanim, a woman of Circassian origin. She was tutored at home and was proficient in French, but learned enough Arabic to memorize the Qur'an (Badran 1995b: 44–46).

10. Malak Hifni Nasif, born 1886 and died 1918, was a feminist activist

and writer, known by the pen name Bahithat al-Badiya (Researcher of the Desert). The daughter of a scholar, she entered primary school when the state opened a section for girls in 1895, and received a diploma in 1901. She also enrolled in the Teachers' Training Program at Saniyah School and received a certificate in 1905. After marriage she published and lectured. She sent a list of feminist demands to the Egyptian Congress in 1911 (Badran 1995c: 229–230).

11. Through African-American, Asian-American, Arab-American and Native-American women's voices and voices from the non-Western world, discussion of different feminisms is gaining momentum in scholarly debates and activist forums. The dominance of the Western model of feminism is being challenged.

12. It is mentioned in Sha'rawi's *Memoirs* that she secretly bought (run-of-the-mill) novels from women peddlers—her only Arabic reading (see Kahf 1998 for an analysis of the *Memoirs* as literature). Kahf notes how the first eleven chapters of the *Memoirs* "tell the story of the journey to acquisition of voice by the girl who had been left outside the door of Arabic self-articulation (1998: 65). The question is: what was the role of Huda's secretary, Abd al-Hamid Fahmi Mursi? Was he a passive ghostwriter or a subordinate "editor" of her verbally transmitted chronicle? The latter is the more likely. In 1892 *Al-'Afaf* started as one in a series of Arabic women's journals, and *al-Fatat* edited by Hind Nawfal, was another. By 1919 over thirty of these periodicals had circulated in Egypt.

13. Badran 1995a describes how, in the second half of the nineteenth century, Egypt experienced growing encroachment by the West on its economic life. The country had become a major source of raw cotton for England following the loss of supplies during the American Civil War. In 1882, the British occupied Egypt on the pretext of safeguarding the khedive and foreign economic interests during the "'Urabi Revolution," a peasant revolt led by 'Urabi Pasha and Egyptian military officers seeking access to the higher ranks monopolized by the Turco-Circassian ruling elite and a broader integration of Egyptians into the civil administration (1995a: 11).

14. Huda's mother participated in establishing a clinic sponsored by the first Lady Cromer (Sha'rawi 1981: 119–120).

15. These were: *Tarqiyat al-Mar'a* (1908), *al-'Afaf* (1892), and *Fatat al-Nil* (1913).

16. These were: *al-Jins al-Latif* (1908) and *al-Sufur* (1915). The writer and editor Abd al-Hamid Hamdi founded the latter, which endorsed complete unveiling, progress and reform in all domains (1915: 1(1), 1, 2).

17. The selections from Qasim Amin were in Badran's book *Feminists, Islam, and Nation* (1995a). I checked them against the original and

retranslated the extracts myself to capture nuances lost in Badran's translation.

18. Egyptians were "lazy and always fleeing work," left their children "covered with dirt and roaming the alleys rolling in the dust like the children of animals," and were sunk in apathy, afflicted, as he put it, "with a paralysis of nerves so that we are unmoved by anything, however beautiful or terrible" (1976, Vol. 2: 134). Nevertheless, over and above such differences between Muslim nationals, Amin asserted, the observer would find both Turks and Egyptians "equal in ignorance, laziness and backwardness" (1976, Vol. 2: 72).

19. This observation is made in the article by Beth Baron (1989: 379)

20. Ahmed 1992 observes that analysts (e.g. Cole 1981: 394–407) routinely treat the debate as one between "feminists," that is, Amin and his allies, and "antifeminists," that is, Amin's critics. They accept at face value the equation made by Amin and the originating Western narrative: the veil signified oppression; therefore those who called for its abandonment were feminist and those opposing its abandonment were antifeminists (Ahmed 1992: 162).

21. Among the dominant political groups finding voice in the press at the time Amin's work was published was a group that strongly supported the British administration and advocated the adoption of a "European outlook." Prominent among its members were a number of Syrian Christians, who founded the pro-British daily *Al-Muqattam*. At the other extreme was a group whose views, articulated in the newspaper *Al-Mu'ayyad*, published by Sheikh 'Ali Yusuf, fiercely opposed Western encroachment in any form and were emphatic about the importance of preserving Islamic tradition in all areas. The National Party (Al-Hizb al-Watani), a group led by Mustapha Kamil, was equally fierce in its opposition to the British and to Westernization, but it espoused a position of secular rather than Islamic nationalism. This group held that advancement for Egypt must begin with the expulsion of the British.

Other groups, including the Umma Party (People's Party), which was to emerge as the politically dominant party in the first decades of the twentieth century, advocated moderation and an attitude of judicious discrimination in identifying political and cultural goals. Muhammad 'Abdu was an important intellectual influence on the Umma Party, though its members were more secular minded; he had advocated the acquisition of Western technology and knowledge and, simultaneously, the revivification and reform of the Islamic heritage, including reform in areas affecting women. The Umma Party advocated the adoption of the European notion of the nation-state in place of religion as the basis of community. Their goals were to adopt Western political institutions and, at the same time, gradually to bring about Egypt's independence from the British. Umma Party members, unlike Mustapha Kamil's ultranationalists or the Islamic nationalists, consequently had an attitude, not of hostility to the British, but rather of measured collaboration. Among its prominent members were Ahmad Lutfi al-Sayyid and Sa'd Zaghloul (Ahmed 1992: 144–168).

To sum up the various political ideological trends, there were: (1) that which supported Europeanization and British colonialism; (2) that which opposed Western encroachment and reaffirmed tradition and Islam; (3) that which opposed colonialism and Westernization, choosing a secular path; and (4) that which called for adopting Western technology and knowledge but chose to revitalize Islamic heritage, and reform women's position.

22. Sulayman al-Salimi, *Didd al 'Afaf* (Against Virtue), Vol. 1, No. 28 (29 May 1911: 14). This is cited in Baron 1989: 383.

23. A contemporary, yet opposite, of Zaynab al-Ghazali in that the former had internalized the superiority of Europe and European ways.

24. Kahf's notion of the *hijab*'s two layers of meaning, concealment versus covering, is polemical and analytically unproductive (1998: 79).

25. Baron, like many writers, makes a link between women's veiling, seclusion, and the "harem system." This linkage hinders analysis. She mistakenly interprets Huda Sha'rawi's dramatic unveiling as "the signal for the end of the harem system" (1989: 371).

26. Here I disagree with Baron, who suggested that the dramatic unveiling act may have been "a significant gesture only to those of the elite" (1989:371).

27. A 1910 photograph in the collection of *al-Mathaf al-Markazi al-Qawmi li-Buhuth al-Tarbiya* (the Central National Museum for Educational Research), of *Wizarat al-Tarbiya* (the Ministry of Education) in Cairo shows students from Abbas girls' school with their faces uncovered. This was noted in Baron 1989.

28. Aflaha Tullab al-Sufur, *al-'Afaf*, 1 (20), 24 March 1911. This is noted in Baron 1989.

29. A photograph taken during the 1919 Revolution shows an unveiled schoolgirl addressing the crowd (Shaarawi 1987: 115).

30. This was in a taped interview I recorded with feminist Ceza al-Nabarawi, a contemporary of Huda Sha'rawi, in February 1979 during our participation in the Symposium, "The Changing Role of Sudanese Women," held in Khartoum, Sudan (22–28 February 1979), in celebration of the 75th anniversary of the founding of Al-Ahfad Schools and Girls' Education.

31. *Izar* is a piece of white calico that covers the whole body like the *habara*, which for a married woman is made of glossy black silk. According to *A Dictionary of Islam* (Hughes 1885) the *izar* is worn by "females of the middle classes, who cannot afford to purchase a *habara*" (1885: 95). This latter comment indeed cannot be applic-

able in this case, since Huda Sha'rawi was a wealthy woman from a family belonging to the gentry of Egypt. Most probably, *izar* was used to refer to the more casual attire worn in non-ceremonial outings.

32. However, the biculturalism of Sha'rawi does not translate into "valorization" of everything European. Her *Memoirs* reveal occasional reluctance to participate in some European social activities. Her Europeanization was not total. She was caught between what is culturally proper and the emblematics of her class.

33. The term used in the *Memoirs* is *al-umam al-raqiya*. *Raqiya* is the same term often used to denote the upper class in Egypt at the time, *al-tabaqa al-raqiya*, meaning the "refined stratum." Classist connotations to the usage are to be noted.

34. Earl Cromer, *Modern Egypt*, 2 vols. (New York: Macmillan, 1908, Vol. 2: 146), cited in Ahmed 1992.

35. For a sophisticated critique of individuated gender and its relation to the Western notion of equality as both relate to feminism see Nelson and Olesen 1977.

36. I have been working on this concept since I began my fieldwork on the Islamic movement in Egypt, which began in the 1970s (El Guindi 1981, 1982a, 1983, 1987, 1992, 1996).

37. This is separate and different from the Society of Muslim Sisters (*al-Akhawat al-Muslimat*), a branch organization of the Muslim Brothers. According to Ahmed "women who joined the [Society of Muslim Sisters] wore a head covering," but the position of the organization differed little from the general modernist position (1992: 194).

38. The Muslim Brothers (*al-Ikhwan al-Muslimin*), founded by Hassan el-Banna (1906–1949) in Egypt in 1928. The Muslim Brothers' platform was anti-colonial, anti-Zionist, and anti-Westernization; it was led by the son of a mosque imam who had studied at al-Azhar and was posted to teach in the Suez Canal town of Ismailia. Al-Banna saw the large disparity between rich and poor lifestyles and the language of foreign domination and injustice that permeated Egypt. He founded the organization on principles of purifying Islam, liberating Egypt and Palestine, and opposing Western-influenced parties and government. It was a grass-roots organization that granted needed services to the underprivileged sectors of the population. It grew rapidly. Al-Banna early on emphasized the important role of women in Islamic reform (Mitchell 1969).

39. The bias built into secularist scholarship is not addressed. It raised the question for my theoretical formulation of feminism of whether an individual Muslim woman's personal experiences (childhood abuse or rape) or ideological positions (such as atheism) qualify her formulations to enter a culture-free spectrum of feminisms? To what

extent is one individual's account of abuse only that? To what extent does an atheist position prejudice discussion on religion? The case of the Bangladeshi physician/writer Taslima Nasrin comes to mind.

References

Ahmed, Leila. 1992. *Women and Gender in Islam: Historical Roots of A Modern Debate*. New Haven, CT: Yale University Press.

Amin, Qasim. 1976 [1900]. *Al-A'mal al-Kamilah li-Qasim Amin* (Complete Works of Qasim Amin), Vol. 2, *al-Mar'a al-Gadida (The New Woman)*, reprinted and compiled in 'Amarah's work, ed. Muhammad 'Amarah, pp. 115–230. Beirut: al-Mu'assasa al-'Arabiyya lil-Dirasat wal-Nashr.

Badran, Margot. 1995a. *Feminists, Islam, and Nation: Gender and the Making of Modern Egypt*. Princeton, NJ: Princeton University Press.

Badran, Margot. 1995b. "Huda Sha'rawi," in John L. Esposito (ed.), *The Oxford Encyclopedia of the Modern Islamic World*, Vol. 4. New York and Oxford: Oxford University Press.

Badran, Margot. 1995c. "Malak Hifni Nasif (1886–1918)," in John L. Esposito (ed.), *The Oxford Encyclopedia of the Modern Islamic World*, Vol. 3. New York and Oxford: Oxford University Press.

Baron, Beth. 1989. "Unveiling in Early Twentieth-Century Egypt: Practical and Symbolic Considerations," *Middle Eastern Studies* 25(3) (July): 370–386.

Barraclough, Steven. 1998. "Al-Azhar: Between the Government and The Islamists," *The Middle East Journal* 52(2) (Spring): 236–250.

Chatty, Dawn. 1997. "The Burqa Face Cover: An Aspect of Dress in Southeastern Arabia," in N. Lindisfarne-Tapper and Bruce Ingham (eds) *Languages of Dress in the Middle East*, pp. 149–177. London: Curzon with The Centre of Near and Middle Eastern Studies, SOAS.

Cole, Juan Ricardo. 1981. "Feminism, Class, and Islam in Turn-of-the-Century Egypt," *International Journal of Middle East Studies* 13(4): 394–407.

Cromer, Earl. 1908. *Modern Egypt, 2 vols*. New York: Macmillan.

Early, Evelyn A. 1993. *Baladi Women of Cairo: Playing with an Egg and a Stone*. Boulder, CO and London: Lynne Rienner Publs.

El Guindi, Fadwa. 1981. "Veiling Infitah with Muslim Ethic: Egypt's Contemporary Islamic Movement," *Social Problems* 28(4): 465–485.

——. 1982a. "From Consciousness to Activism: Dynamics of the Islamic Movement," American Research Center Lecture Series. Cairo: ARCE Office.

——. 1982b. "Die Ruckkehr zum Schleier: Vom unaufhaltsamen Siegeszug eins konservativen Symbols. Nahost in Flammen," *Der Monat*(285): 165–178.

——. 1983. "Veiled Activism: Egyptian Women in the Contemporary Islamic Movement,' *Peuples Mediterranéans* (Femmes de la Mediterranée) 22–23: 79–89.

——. 1985. "The Status of Women in Bahrain: Social and Cultural Considerations," in J. Nugent and T. Thomas (eds) *Bahrain and the Gulf*, pp. 75–95. Sydney: Croom Helm.

——. 1986. "The Egyptian Woman: Trends Today, Alternatives Tomorrow," in Lynne B. Iglitzin and Ruth Ross (eds) *Women in the World, 1975–1985: The Women's Decade*, pp. 225–242. Santa Barbara, California: ABC-CLIO.

——. 1987. "Das islamische Kleid 'al-hidschab'," in G. Volger, K. V. Welck and K. Hackstein (eds) *Pracht und Geheimnis: Kleidung und Schmuck aus Palästina und Jordanie*, pp. 164–167. Cologne: Rautenstrauch-Joest-Museim der Stadt Koln.

——. 1992. "Feminism Comes of Age in Islam," *Los Angeles Times* (Op-Ed).

——. 1996. "Feminism Comes of Age in Islam," in Suha Sabbagh (ed.), *Arab Women: Between Defiance and Restraint*, pp. 159–161. New York: Olive Branch Press.

——. 1997. "Islamic Identity and Resistance," Middle East Institute Annual Conference. National Press Club, Washington DC, Friday, 3 October.

——. 1998. "Gender in Islamic Activism: The Case of Egypt," McLean, Virginia, 21 May.

El-Messiri, Sawsan. 1978. "Self Images of Traditional Urban Women in Cairo," in L. Beck and N. Keddie (eds) *Women in Muslim Society*, pp. 522–557. Cambridge, MA: Harvard University Press.

Fernea, Elizabeth W. and Basima Q. Bezirgan. 1977. "Huda Sha'rawi: Founder of the Egyptian Women's Movement," in Elizabeth W. Fernea and Basima Q. Bezirgan (eds), *Middle Eastern Muslim Women Speak*, pp. 193–200. Austin and London: University of Texas Press.

Ghazali, Zaynab al-. 1977. *Ayam min Hayati* (Days from My Life) (Arabic). Cairo and Beirut: Dar al-Shuruq.

Goldschmidt, A. Jr. 1983. *A Concise History of the Middle East*. Boulder, Co: Westview Press.

Harb, Tal'at. 1905 [1899]. *Tarbiyet al-Mar'a wa al-hijab (Socialization of Women and the Veil)*. Cairo: Matba'at al-Manar.

Hoffman, Valerie J. 1985. "An Islamic Activist: Zeinab al-Ghazali," in Elizabeth W. Fernea (ed.) *Women and the Family in the Middle East: New Voices of Change*. Austin, TX: University of Texas Press.

Hoffman-Ladd, Valerie J. 1995. "Zaynab Al-Ghazali," in John L. Esposito (ed.), *The Oxford Encyclopedia of the Modern Islamic World*, Vol. 2. New York, Oxford: Oxford University Press.

Hughes, T. Patrick (ed.) (1885). "Dress," in idem, *A Dictionary of Islam*, pp. 92–99. Lahore: Premier Book House Publishers and Booksellers.

Kahf, Mohja. 1998. "Huda Sha'rawi's Mudhakkirati: The Memoirs of the First Lady of Arab Modernity," *Arab Studies Quarterly* 20(1) (Winter): 53–82.

Khalidi, 'Anbara Salam al-. 1978. *Jawla fil-Thikrayat bayna Lubnan wa-Falastin* (A Journey of Memories from Lebanon to Palestine). Beirut.

Marsot, Afaf L. al-Sayyid. 1978. "The Revolutionary Gentlewomen in Egypt," in L. Beck and N. Keddie (eds) *Women in the Muslim World*, pp. 261–276. Cambridge, MA: Harvard University Press.

Marsot, Afaf L. al-Sayyid, (ed.). 1979. *Society and the Sexes in Medieval Islam*. Malibu, CA: Undena Publications.

Mernissi, Fatima. 1975. *Beyond the Veil: Male-Female Dynamics in a Modern Muslim Society*. Cambridge: Schlenkman.

Mir-Hosseini, Ziba. 1996. "Women and Politics in Post-Khomeini Iran: Divorce, Veiling and Emergent Feminist Voices', in Haleh Afshar (ed.), *Women and Politics in the Third World*, pp. 142–170. London & New York: Routledge.

Mitchell, Richard P. 1969. *The Society of the Muslim Brothers*. London: Oxford University Press.

Nabarawi, Ceza al-. 1979. Khartoum, Sudan, February: tape-recorded interview.

Nasif, Malak Hifni. 1909. *Nisa'iyyat (Feminist Texts)*. Cairo: Al-Jarida Press.

Nasif, Majd al-Din Hifni. 1962. *Athar Bahithat al-Badiyah Malak Hifni Nasif: 1886–1918* (The Influence of Bahithat al-Badiya Malak Hifni Nasif: 1886–1918). Cairo: Wizarat al-Thaqafah wa-al-Irshad al-Qawmi.

Nelson, Cynthia. 1974. "Public and Private Politics: Women in the Middle Eastern World," *American Ethnologist* 1: 551–563.

——. 1996. *Doria Shafiq the Feminist: A Woman Apart*. Cairo: American University in Cairo Press.

Nelson, Cynthia and Virginia Olesen. 1977. "Veil of Illusion: A Critique of the Concept of Equality in Western Feminist Thought," *Catalyst* 10–11: 8–36.

Norton, J. 1997. "Faith and Fashion in Turkey," in N. Lindisfarne-Tapper and Bruce Ingham (eds), *Languages of Dress in the Middle East*, pp. 149–177. London: Curzon with The Centre of Near and Middle Eastern Studies, SOAS.

Olson, E. A. 1985. "Muslim Identity and Secularism in Contemporary Turkey: 'The Headscarf Dispute'," *Anthropological Quarterly* 58(4): 161–171.

Quataert, Donald. 1997. "Clothing Laws, State, and Society in the Ottoman Empire, 1720–1829," *International Journal of Middle East Studies* 29: 403–425.

Rashid, Fatima. 1908a. "Kalima 'an al-Hal al-Hadira (A Word on the Present Condition)," *Tarqiyat al-Mar'a*, 1 (5).

——. 1908b. "al-Hijab," *Tarqiyat al-Mar'a*, 1 (6).

Sayyid-Marsot, Afaf Lutfi al-. 1995. *Women and Men in Late Eighteenth-Century Egypt*, Modern Middle East Series. Austin, TX: University of Texas Press.

Shaarawi, Huda. 1987. *Harem Years: The Memoirs of an Egyptian Feminist (1879–1924)*, trans. Margot Badran. New York: The Feminist Press.

Sha'rawi, Huda. 1981. *Huda Sharawi: Muthakkirat Ra'idat al-Mar'a al-Arabiyya al-Hadith* (Memoirs of Huda Sharawy, Leader of Modern Arab Women) (Introduction by Amina al-Said) (Arabic), Kitab al-Hilal, Silsila Shahriyya. Cairo: Dar al-Hilal.

Wallace, Anthony F. C. 1956. "Revitalization Movements," *American Anthropologist* 58: 264–281.

Fashion Theory, Volume 3, Issue 1, pp.81–108
Reprints available directly from the Publishers.
Photocopying permitted by licence only.
© 1999 Berg. Printed in the United Kingdom.

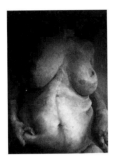

Mar(k)ing the Objected Body: A Reading of Contemporary Female Tattooing

Michael Hardin

Michael Hardin received his
Ph.D. in American Literature
from the University of Houston
where he now teaches. He
has published widely on
contemporary literature and
culture. He is currently
finishing work on two books,
*Playing the Reader: The
Homoerotics of Self-Reflexive
Fiction* and *Devouring
Institutions: The Life Work of
Kathy Acker*.

"But nice girls don't get tattooed."

—Samuel Steward

"There's always something terribly flawed about people who are tattooed."

—Truman Capote

Introduction

Recently, tattooing has become a faddish part of contemporary counter culture and has been appropriated by those outside the stereotypical "tattooed" populations—"[p]rofessional criminals, outlaw motor-cyclists, users of illegal drugs, prostitutes, those that identify with 'punk' culture and other members of counter-conventional subcultures" (Sanders 1989: 238). However, the present popularity of tattooing does not mean that it has become an accepted aspect of Western culture; it is still seen as "other" despite its increasing popularity. One reason for the hesitation in embracing tattooing can be traced to the West's Judeo-Christian roots: "Do not cut your bodies for the dead or put tattoo marks on yourselves" (Leviticus 19.28, *NIV*). This emphasis on the "purity" of the body is furthered in the New Testament: "For we are the temple of the living God" (2 Corinthians 6.16, *NIV*). For women, bodily "purity" is an even greater demand because the woman, throughout Western history, has been the object of the male aesthetic; this is most evident when one examines one of the most popular and consistent subjects of art, the female nude.

> Women, who for centuries had been the *objects* of male theorizing, male desires, male fears and male representations, had to discover and reappropriate themselves as *subjects* . . . The call went out to invent both a new poetics and a new politics, based on women's reclaiming what had always been theirs but had been usurped from them: control over their bodies and a voice with which to speak about it (Suleiman 1985: 7).

The reclamation of the body provides the means for the woman to alter the objectification of the female and to establish a space from which to speak. By inscribing the text on the body, the woman forces the male to recognize the body as text, but by tattooing the body the woman "mar(k)s" the object, and thus denies the male the pleasure he receives from dictating and admiring his own standard of beauty and "devalues" the commodified object of masculine economy. The tattoo becomes the sign of the woman's recognition of the historic and violent imposition of the male cultural narrative upon the female, the denial of the woman's place as his object in that narrative, the removal of herself from the patriarchal exchange, and the presentation of a new and individual, female narrative, which by being inscribed upon the body, cannot be appropriated.

A History of Tattooing in the West

Tattooing is an ancient ritual that has been found in the traditions of Africa, the Americas, Asia, and Oceania. According to one source, the word *tattoo* itself can be traced to the Polynesian word '*tatau*,' which originally meant "right," "straight," or "skilled" (Weideger 1986: 85). This original definition indicates a radically different view of tattooing than is currently held in North America and Europe. What is counter culture in the West is "right" or "straight" elsewhere; it is a "skilled" activity. Samuel Steward, an English professor turned tattoo artist, suggests that the modern Christian prohibitions against tattooing may be ungrounded:

> In the Talmud and elsewhere it has been claimed that Christ . . . tattooed the magic word for Jehovah [Yahweh] on his thigh . . . But Christianity stopped the "barbarous practice" of tattooing at least for a while, and set up the prejudice against it which has existed ever since the Ecumenical Council of Nicaea in 787 A.D., during which Pope Hadrian I declared a ban against it (Steward 1990: 186).

Because it can never be proven either way, the idea that Christ was tattooed is less important than Hadrian I's papal edict; the fact that an edict was needed seems to indicate that tattooing was a common enough practice for the Pope to feel that he needed to intervene. What this edict indicates is that tattooing is a repressed part of Christian history, not merely an "exotic" or "barbarous" practice of "primitive" cultures; it seems as if the practice of tattooing went underground at this point. According to Rubin, with the exception of a few cult or sect appearances, tattooing was not known or practiced on a significant scale in Europe until the late fifteenth century, when the Europeans began their explorations in Asia, Africa, and the Americas (Rubin 1988: 14). Steward does not indicate how widespread the practice was in early European history, but he does say that tattooing was practiced by the Celts, Picts, and Gauls before the imposition of Christianity, and later by the Norse, Danes, and Saxons, who would tattoo their family crests on their bodies (Steward 1990: 185). It was not until the end of the eighteenth and the beginning of the nineteenth centuries that interest in and involvement with tattooing among Europeans and North Americans began expanding; this was due primarily to the sailors and travelers who were returning from Indochina, Indonesia, Japan, Micronesia, and Polynesia with intricate and detailed designs on their bodies (Rubin 1988: 14). However, this increased knowledge of tattooing did not help bridge the gulf between cultures, but in fact widened it; the Europeans and North Americans used tattooing as a basis on which to establish their sense of cultural superiority—because they did not practice it, they were superior (Rubin 1988: 14). Tattooing was a sign of the exotic, "primitive," or "Oriental."

As colonies began to receive their independence after the Second World War this cultural hierarchy regarding tattooing slowly began to lessen; independence forced their former colonizers to acknowledge "their right to seek for themselves the benefits of participation in the modern world" (Rubin 1988: 14). As independent societies, their cultural practices were no longer seen merely as the actions of ignorant and savage tribes (although some would and do still feel this way), but as the cultural capital of a society capable of governing itself and existing in the global community. (However, these people are still marginalized as "Third World" or "pre-Industrial.") With the advent, in the 1960s, of the Peace Corps and similar European organizations, as well as the "Hippie Movement," tattooing evolved in importance and practice among the populations of Western countries (Rubin 1988: 14). The Peace Corps allowed Americans to experience foreign cultures in a new manner: no longer were they coming merely as tourists or colonizers to sanitized or exotic environments, but they were now encountering a more accurate sense of what the culture truly was (Rubin 1988: 14). I would argue that they still came as outsiders and imposed their own narrative on the cultural rituals and signs, and appropriated what they found. They took the sign, the tattoo, apparently without much interest in its ritual function or meaning. The Hippie Movement represented an expansion of consciousness that reflected its exposure to non-European, principally Native American and Asian, attitudes toward the body (Rubin 1988: 16). This hippie shift in body politics is an affront to the Judeo-Christian tradition which has man made in the image of God. To change the "image of God" is to separate oneself from God, or in a more radical sense, to be read as blasphemous.

This antagonism between world-views and body politics seems to be one of the driving forces in the contemporary philosophy of tattooing. As the traditional master-narratives are being discounted and dismissed, people are searching for new, localized narratives: personal narratives that they can express on themselves, personal narratives that express their control over themselves. "During the 1970's, Women's Liberation and Gay Liberation asserted—even celebrated—people's control over their own bodies, sometimes expressed in anathematized forms of body art" (Rubin 1988: 15). At this point, marginalized groups seeking power were using the tattoo and other forms of body art as a means to express their fight for their bodies on the very site of that contest. Women, lesbians and gays, as well as people of color, have been subjected to control by the dominant society/gender/sexual orientation/skin color over their bodies or because of their bodies. Women's bodies have been controlled by the male as either virgin mothers or whores: the male wants to protect/confine to the home the sexless wife/mother/daughter while he wants to gaze at/objectify/commodify the sexual woman.[1] The lesbian or gay is discriminated against because what she or he accepts as normal sexuality is considered aberrant, if not illegal, by the heterosexual body politic, and thus there is an attempt to regulate, closet, or restrict the lesbian or gay body. The person of color's body is the site of control or restriction because of its color; the color of one's skin/body is used as an excuse to control or monitor that person's actions. If the body is the site of, or reason for, control, then it seems that the body itself would be the most subversive and thus most appropriate space for voice and reaction.

The body becomes the appropriate space of reaction because for so long it has been the site of appropriation; by marking the body of one who has been placed outside the social order because of his/her body, one can challenge the very legitimization of that order, or refuse to be the defining "other." In his major work on body art, Michel Thévoz states that tattooing is one of the ways that marginalized people "speak": "tattooing is in fact often resorted to by those who cannot easily express themselves in words, who confusedly feel themselves the victims of the logocentric order and react spectacularly by infringing the cultural principles of body integrity" (Thévoz 1984: 80). It goes without saying that women, ethnic and racial minorities, and lesbians and gays are victimized by the logocentric and phallogocentric orders of Western cultures at the site of the body. Jane Marcus, in her critique of carnivalism in Djuna Barnes' *Nightwood*, argues that

> [w]riting on the body . . . is breaking a powerful patriarchal taboo for the inheritors of the Judeo-Christian ethos in which the possession of the Logos is indicated by writing on the holy tablets. Making human skin into a page of text violates the symbolic order. A body covered with marks is too close to the natural "unclean" state of the newborn's body, which bears the marks of the "unclean" placenta, the traces of its mother's blood. A tattoo, then, is not only taboo; it is also a birthmark of the born-again—the self-created person who denies his or her birth identity (Marcus 1991: 222–3).

The challenge that tattooing seems to hold for Marcus is twofold: first, it gives the person possession of the Word, the Logos, which is the basis for the Law of the Fathers; secondly, it situates the person, bearing the Word on his/her body, in a state of uncleanness. Tattooing not only mar(k)s the body, but it defiles the Word/Law. Given this rather significant challenge to the patriarchal hegemony, tattooing seems appropriate for the person who is marginalized by the Word to subvert it through the incorporation of the Word into his/her own skin. The culture will be forced to confront both the "expressed" Word and the "suppressed" body at the same time, and ideally will see the effect the former has upon the latter.

The Tattooing of Women across Cultures

Although there is little documentation of tattooing among women in pre-modern and contemporary Europe and North America, there is rather extensive information on the tattooing of women in other cultures.

In his extensive study, *The History of Tattooing and Its Significance: With Some Account of Other Forms of Corporal Marking*, W. D. Hambly provides what he believes is the meaning of the tattooing of women: "In addition to being the signs of womanhood and a marriageable age, the marks probably form part of the mysticism which is necessary for launching the maiden forth into the higher dignities attaching to the office of wife and mother" (Hambly 1925: 211). The way in which Hambly reads the tattooing is that it is a sign marking a girl's entrance into womanhood that mystically aids her in the process of her achieving the "higher dignity" of wife and mother. This reading, especially the second half of it, is noticeably prejudiced in its attributing status to the woman's position only in her relationship to the man. In Hambly's entire study, he is always an outsider looking in and providing meaning for ritual actions that he cannot fully understand. Instead of providing the possibility that tattooing of women at this age could be an act related to menstrual bleeding or a female rite of passage or some other occurrence that happens at that time in a woman's life, he assumes it is related to marriage and the resultant attainment of social status. He may well be correct in his reading, but his refusal to allow for other options still places him in the role of the outsider imposing a cultural narrative. Another example of how he reads cultural phenomena comes during a discussion of the Fiji practice of tattooing women's buttocks, which he says "has undoubtedly some hidden sexual significance" (Hambly 1925: 215). His willingness to say "undoubtedly" and "hidden . . . significance" in the same sentence reveals his lack of access to tribal ritual meaning, yet he still draws conclusions without that information. However, this imposition of meaning is what I will later argue is the very thing that contemporary Western female tattooing may be a reaction against; the woman, by being tattooed, is acknowledging the historic impositions by the male power structure on the female body, but is then reclaiming her own body, rewriting her own narrative, and recreating her own meaning.

In his "Introduction: Oceania," in *Marks of Civilization: Artistic Transformations of the Human Body*, Arnold Rubin cites a Samoan origin myth of tattooing. According to the myth, two women deities, originally Siamese twins, were given an order to take to the people of Samoa: *tatau fafine, ae le tatau tane* (tattoo the women, but don't tattoo the men) (Rubin 1988: 155). However, while they were swimming toward Samoa and repeating this phrase, they saw on the ocean bottom a tridachna shell and dove to retrieve it. When they surfaced, they began repeating their order again, but now it came out as *tatau tane, ae le tatau fafine* (tattoo men, but don't tattoo the women) (Rubin 1988: 155). In 1969, Milner provided the following explanation of the myth:

> The function of tattooing . . . is to restore the balance between the sexes. Or to put it in Levi-Straussian terms, the institution of

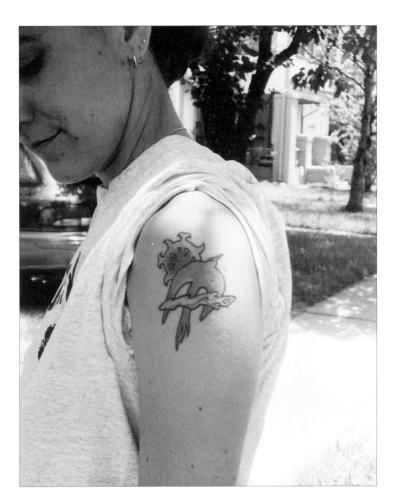

Figure 1
Martha Serpas.

tattooing mediates between nature and culture, man and women, pleasure and pain, life and death, and is typified by a monster in the shape of two female Siamese twins, joined back to back, whose function is to give pain to man and joy to woman to a degree which is notionally equivalent to the pain that childbirth gives to woman and to the joy childbirth gives to man (cited by Rubin 1988: 155).

Milner states that in this myth tattooing cancels the differences between the sexes, as well as the differences between nature and culture, pleasure and pain, and life and death. "Eradicating the difference between the sexes" is what Irigaray argues is the function of phallocentric discourse, which removes the female altogether from the language. By this reading, the role of the woman disappears; it is only the role of the tattooed male that remains. Milner seems to increase the difference by reading the two women as a "monster" and by suggesting that the pain endured by tattooing is equal to the pain endured by a woman during childbirth. The consequence of this reading seems to be a decreasing in the importance of the cultural role of woman without any similar decrease in the role of man. Man, by merely being tattooed, has usurped any social or cultural power and importance that a woman would otherwise have due to her role as mother. Milner's reading is further problematized by the original dictum of the deities: tattoo the women but not the men. If this supposed gender and cosmic equality was derived from this myth, then it was arrived at accidentally; why was the original command to tattoo only women if it was meant to balance out experiences of pain and joy? Again, it seems as if this myth is crudely interpreted to fit a Taoist type of philosophy without that interpretation being overtly apparent within the text.

In some of the more recent investigations into the tattooing of women, the research focuses more on describing the tattoos, their locations, and what the wearers say the significance of the tattooing is. In "The Spiritual Significance of Newar Tattoos," Jehanne Teilhet-Fisk describes the practice by the Newar women (indigenous Nepalese) of drawing and inscribing their own designs. The Newar women create their own designs, generally on their lower legs so that they would be visible below their sarongs, and put them on the body themselves. If help is needed in the process, such as to reach certain places on the leg, other women are called to help; the only males who would ever be permitted to help in this process are the brothers of the mother (Teilhet-Fisk 1988: 135). The exclusion of men in this process for a tattoo that is to be seen publicly suggests that there is some meaning or ritual for women in the act itself; unfortunately, that meaning or ritual importance is not given. However, there are two reasons which are given for the tattooing by the Newar women: the first is that the tattooing is seen as beautiful, and the second is a belief that "they must have some wound" (Teilhet-Fisk 1988: 138–9). Teilhet-Fisk records two statements by Newar women who both mention the importance of the wound and the luck or good fortune it brings: "'The wound will bring us good luck in the next life. Tattooing gives us some pain and it leaves a permanent mark; this will give us good luck'"; "'It is beautiful and it is necessary to have a wound in this life because it will be good for the next life. Also the tattoos will not fade and it is said that when one dies, who has been tattooed, that person can sell their tattoos in the heavens'" (Teilhet-Fisk 1988: 139). The tattoo is a mark of beauty, pain, and permanence; the tattoo, inscribed by the woman herself and/or other women, will be one thing which lasts, not only throughout her life, but also into the afterlife. The tattoo becomes the cultural sign that crosses all barriers: it does not reveal social status; it is a permanent embellishment and is thus an intrinsic sign of the individual; and, it is not a prerogative for any class, marital status, or gender—males may also be tattooed (Teilhet-Fisk 1988: 139).

Teilhet-Fisk's analysis provides a type of heterogeneous space, a leveling of difference; this sets her apart from Thévoz, who has his own theoretical point to put forth. He argues, very generally, that tattooing is the mark of the symbolic order that is designed to prevent leveling or any sense of equality within a society (Thévoz 1984: 61). Obviously, the specificity of Teilhet-Fisk's study gives it a validity which the generality of Thévoz's cannot provide; so, at least in the case of the Newar women, tattooing appears to be a sign of a lack of difference.

Moving from Non-Western to Western Tattooing of Women via Freud and Irigaray

The reason that the Newar women feel it is important to be tattooed so that they may have a wound reflects a very non-Western, non-Freudian view of the female body; they do not suffer from a culturally imposed "castration complex," the idea that the vagina is a wound where a penis should be. Luce Irigaray describes the consequences of the "castration complex" on the female:

> Woman's castration is defined as her having nothing you can see, as her *having* nothing. In her having nothing penile, in seeing that she has No Thing. Nothing *like* man. That is to say *no sex/organ* that can be seen in a *form* capable of founding its reality, reproducing its truth. *Nothing to be seen is equivalent to having no thing. No being* and *no truth*. The contract, the collusion, between *one* sex/organ and the victory won by the visual dominance therefore leaves woman with her sexual void, with an "actual castration" carried out in actual fact (Irigaray 1985b: 48).

By seeing the vagina as the wound from castration, the woman is forced into a position of inferiority, of lack, of non-being, and ultimately, of "actual castration." For the Newar woman, the wound is a beautiful embellishment and asset; it acknowledges a visual cultural aesthetic in which the "marked" body is beautiful.[2] For the contemporary Western woman, the tattoo can also be a way to refute the negative, whorish view of sexuality taken by the traditional white male. By marking the body, the woman acknowledges the "visual dominance" of the culture, but then separates herself from it by confronting the male gaze; no longer is the woman the alabaster Venus of Titian, Botticelli, Goya, or Manet, but is "marked/marred" and is thus "devalued" as the object of the male aesthetic, and so can no longer be the object of male exchange.

While some cultures do use the tattooing of women as a sign of freedom and individuality, in others it is a sign of commodification inscribed upon the woman just prior to her being given to a husband. Among certain Melanesian cultures, a girl, before she was to be married, would be caged from four weeks to twenty months in a *mbak*, an annexe to her parents' house that was so small the girl could not stand, but would be forced to sit or lie. During this period, she would only be able to go out at night, when the elder women of the village would bring her *any* men in the village with whom she wished to have sex. During this period of confinement, she would be tattooed; upon leaving the *mbak*, she would move in with her husband and be expected to be faithful in marriage from then on (Weideger 1986: 116–17). Therefore, the tattooing is associated with her confinement, both in the *mbak* and in the marriage. Claude Lévi-Strauss writes that women are "circulated between clans, lineages, or families, in place of the words of the group, which are circulated among individuals" (Lévi-Strauss 1963: 61). If one can extrapolate from Lévi-Strauss's observations, keeping in mind Irigaray's notion of the *hom(m)o-sexual*, then we can agree that women are exchanged as commodities, and the tattoo then becomes the deed of ownership or the signature of the transaction. According to a former prostitute who worked in Las Vegas in the 1950s, pimps would tattoo their prostitutes, and when a woman went to a new pimp, an X would be placed over the previous pimp's tattoo and a new tattoo would be inscribed. The extent to which tattooed women were considered prostitutes has not been documented, but the responses which have been recorded seem to indicate that prostitutes were the most common or most notorious women who were tattooed: "'Imagine . . . that damfool Sally . . . a-gittin' a *tat*too jes' like a big-city whore!'" (Steward 1990: 130). The prostitute represents the most self-conscious incorporation of "woman as commodity"; as such, by being so associated with tattooing, she allows it to represent the selling of the body, being commodified. Therefore, for the contemporary woman, the tattoo can be read as a recognition of the historic commodification of the female body, but also as an assertion that the body is no longer for sale. There is no longer a pimp or father to sell her body to a john or husband; she owns and controls her body. The tattoo is not the sign of her pimp or her family, but her self.

Tattooing and the Western Beauty Aesthetic

Any analysis of contemporary tattooing must address the beauty aesthetic, which encourages the use of make-up, powder, implants, liposuction, and other body manipulations. Thévoz compares tattooing and scarification with such beauty practices as shaving hair, removing spots, and wearing of corsets (Thévoz 1984: 76–7). Conversely, Marc Blanchard sees a radical difference between permanent and non-permanent body manipulation; at the same time, however, he asserts that women are more interested in the cosmetic aspects of tattooing, while men use tattooing to assert their identity (Blanchard 1994: 292).

What seems to be the difference between tattooing and make-up is not only the permanence but the aesthetic itself: make-up and other cosmetics tend to construct the female body in a manner that fits the visual desire of patriarchal society, while tattooing disrupts the standard Western conventions of beauty.[3]

This disruption is very clear in the responses of men to women with tattoos. Christopher Gotch and Ronald Scutt, in a supposedly unbiased study of tattooing, make some observations that indicate a predilection for a conventional aesthetic with regard to women's appearance: "The fair sex, in general, is not prone to acquiring tattoos . . . For other than those who have been institutionalized, few women approve of tattooing, let alone indulge in it. It would be fair to state that most women who possess tattoos gained them through the influence of their menfolk"

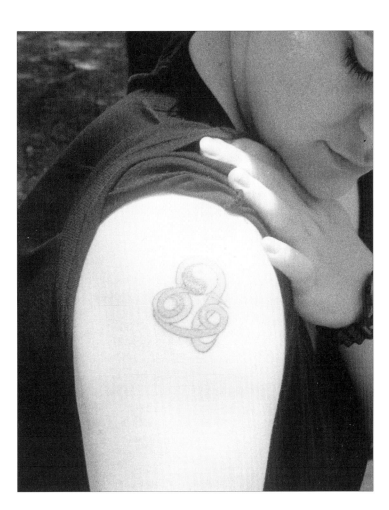

Figure 2
Courtney Rath.

(Gotch and Scutt 1974: 143). This comment came only twenty years ago, and admittedly tattooing among women was rarer than it is today, but tattooing among men was also rarer, at least among non-military and non-prison populations. However, what this quotation shows, by the use of terms such as the "fair sex" to describe women who should not have tattoos and "institutionalized" to describe those who do, is that tattooing is and should be gender-specific. These men do not divulge the evidence which leads to these conclusions, but present their statements as fact. Shortly after the previous statement, they claim that, "[c]ertainly most girls today regard the practice with utter horror, and would never be seen anywhere near a tattoo shop" (Gotch and Scutt 1974: 144). To preface their remark with "certainly" indicates a cavalier attitude towards their subject; they do not even consider that women may want tattoos. They merely presume that women would look upon it with the same horror as they do. They support their argument with an illogical remark by an unnamed man (who himself is tattooed) about why women should not be tattooed: "[i]n Nature you find the male animals with the brightest plumage and the most attractive colors, in order that they can attract the female of the species. This is why most men get tattooed. But I would be strongly suspicious of women who get tattooed. Since they would be offensive to men they must have some other idea in mind" (Gotch and Scutt 1974: 145). This man conflates the ideas of biological determinism with cultural construction in an attempt to explain why men get tattooed and women should not, and the authors of the study do not critique this. What is presented is a reinscription of standard gender roles: the male is free to function as he pleases within the society and pursue the female, who must submit to his aesthetic; if she does not, she is offensive. In yet another telling comment, Scutt and Gotch discuss female tattooing, which they tend to limit to cosmetic tattooing, primarily tattooing whitish pigments into birthmarks. Given this antagonism towards women with tattoos, which is based in the Western aesthetic of female beauty, it would seem unimaginable for women who did get tattooed not to know that they were challenging or subverting that very aesthetic itself.

Blanchard attempts to argue that tattooing is becoming middle-class, and by that I interpret him to mean "mainstream," and his evidence is that the upper class has tattoos and therefore has legitimized it for the middle class (Blanchard 1994: 291). The flaws in his argument are the following: first, he conflates celebrity and upper class—his examples are Madonna and Cher; secondly, he seems to overlook how the middle class actually views these women, more often as immoral than as models of behavior; and lastly, he uses women to support a trend that he claims is happening primarily among men. The women Blanchard cites as examples of upper-class tattooees are sex symbols, and not the traditional members of the upper class. It is nearly impossible to prove middle-class acceptance of tattooing, if, as he suggests, it is primarily a male phenomenon and the models of behavior are sex symbols; this seems to have less to do with class legitimization than with the sexual objectification of women. Blanchard is participating in this objectification by using Madonna and Cher as his example yet refusing to notice that women may be getting more tattoos than men.[4]

Sexuality and the Marked Body

For women, the body has been the site of contention, the space that the dominant society has repeatedly tried to control and monitor. The sexuality of the body, according to Michel Foucault, is one space that has, especially since the nineteenth century, been strictly monitored, repressed, and guarded:

> Sexuality was carefully confined; it moved into the home . . . On the subject of sex, silence became the rule . . . Nothing that was not ordered in terms of generation or transfigured by it could expect sanction or protection. Nor did it merit a hearing. It would be driven out, denied, and reduced to silence. Not only did it not exist, it had no right to exist and would be made to disappear upon its least manifestation—whether in acts or in words (Foucault 1990: 3–4).

It is rather obvious the extent to which sexuality has been repressed and silenced. However, it is women whose sexuality has been most greatly the subject of control and repression: women are reduced by the virgin/whore dichotomy, which allows them only to be idolized as sexless mothers or be demonized as seductive whores. The significance of the tattoo must then be expanded beyond mere textuality to include the sexuality of the body as well; the text of the tattoo should not be limited to the tattoo itself, but should be expanded to include the process, the context, and the body.

In non-Western cultures where tattooing has been the sign of the commodification of the female, it has also been associated with female sexuality, either by the tattooing of the sexual organs or the concurrent actions taken with the tattooing. Among the Ponape of the Caroline Islands, tattooing of the genitalia "starts when the girl is between seven or eight and continues until the age of twelve . . . 'The adornment of the genitalia is so intricate and careful that both the labia majora and vaginal orifice are tattooed'" (Weideger 1986: 88). The girl's entrance into puberty and sexuality is accompanied by her sex organs' being tattooed; what role this tattooing plays is not commented upon. The details which Kubary provides about the Pelew Islanders are more extensive and telling: "So soon as the girl has intimate relations with men, she is decorated with the indispensable *telengekel* (tattooing), otherwise no man would ever look at her. The *telengekel* consists of a triangle which covers the mons veneris, and is bounded by a straight line (*greel*)" (cited by Weideger 1986: 88). The tattooing marks the girl's first encounters with sexuality, and yet without it she would be sexually ostracized. The culture must mark her sex for her to be a sexual member and commodity for exchange. Tattooing is then a requirement if a woman is to have a sexual existence in her society. Kubary mentions that the women of Nukuoro must have tattooed genitalia if they are to become mothers: "'In spite of the sparseness, the tattoo patterns of the Nukuoro are highly important, for all children born to women who have not been tattooed are put to death. Tattooing is the sign of maturity and membership of the community of women'" (cited by Weideger 1986: 88). In this society, tattooing of the genitalia is a requirement for motherhood. The woman's maternal sexuality is denied unless the woman conforms to what seems to be a female rite of passage; it does not appear that the woman would not be accepted sexually by the men, but any resulting children would be killed. For an untattooed woman, sex would carry a death penalty for the child she might conceive. Without a tattoo, the woman would be denied one role which does differentiate the genders and provides some degree of presence in a culture. Among the Vey, during the rites of passage of the girls, they "go about naked in their sandy and on entry are tattooed and undergo clitoridectomy" (Weideger 1986: 110). Tattooing becomes the external sign for the removal of the tip of the clitoris. Gayatri Spivak argues that "the excision, effacement, and symbolic suppression of the clitoris is always an effort to define women in terms of their reproductive function and as objects of sexual exchange, to remove the sign of female sexual autonomy and subjectivity" (Showalter 1990: 131). If we apply Spivak's statement to the Vey, then the tattooing marks the event, the clitoridectomy, that defines the women of the culture by their reproductive function and not as sexually autonomous persons. However, without the tattooing and the clitoridectomy, the woman has no function within the culture. In the Vey, Nukuoro, Pelew, and Ponape cultures, the tattooing of the women effectively functions as, or represents, a control of their sexuality; either the tattooing of the genitalia is part of a rite of passage into womanhood, or the tattooing accompanies a clitoridectomy in the rite of passage. Sexuality and cultural identity are controlled and the tattoo is the external and visible sign that accompanies this control.

Writing the Body

Since the tattooing of women has such a history, it would seem odd that the tattoo could become a representation to which contemporary feminists could be attracted; however, with the current emphasis in feminist theory on the body and the politics of the body, having a text inscribed on the body becomes the perfect image or metaphor, especially for the female writer and theorist, for whom inscription has an added importance. Also, since the suppressive narratives have been written and controlled by the patriarchal structures, it is unknown what the original meaning or significance of the tattooing was.[5] Judith Butler states that the problem of the past generation has been how to bring the feminine body into writing: "a generation of feminist writing . . . tried, with varying degrees of success, to bring the feminine body into writing, to write the feminine proximately or directly, sometimes without even a hint of a preposition or marker of linguistic distance between the writing and the written" (Butler 1993: *ix*). Susan Gubar discusses part of the reason why it has been difficult finding such a feminine writing:

> This model of the pen-penis writing on the virgin page participates in a long tradition identifying the author as male who is primary and the female as his passive creation—a secondary object lacking autonomy, endowed with often contradictory meaning but denied intentionality. Clearly this tradition excludes women from the creation of culture, even as it reifies her as an artifact within culture. It is therefore problematic for those women who want to appropriate the pen and become writers (Gubar 1985: 295).

The woman writer is placed in a paradoxical position: how does she write with the traditional tool, the pen/penis, on the traditional virgin page? Since women have been created as cultural objects by the male artist/writer through the media of painting and writing, the woman writer must find both a new stylus and a new medium or alter the pen to function in a non-impositional manner. The mode some women have begun to adopt involves not abandoning the field altogether but redefining the positions within it, being writer and text, creator and object; the difference is that now she determines the content. She controls the authorial representation of the female. To say she controls the text is to deny the function of the reader; however, by no longer having only male writers or artists create female characters for the pleasure reading/ viewing of the male public, the woman creates a shift in the old economic exchange, what Irigaray terms the *hom(m)o-sexual*, where males no longer maintain absolute control.

If language is inherently phallocentric, then for a woman to subvert the cultural narrative/text, she must alter the language itself. In *This Sex Which Is Not One*, Irigaray explains the position of the woman in both discourse and philosophy:

> this domination of philosophic logos stems in part from its power to *reduce all others to the economy of the Same*. The teleologically constructive project it takes on is always also a project of diversion, deflection, reduction of the other in the Same. And, in its greatest

generality perhaps, from its power to *eradicate the difference between the sexes* in systems that are self-representative of a "masculine subject" (Irigaray 1985a: 74).

Since language and philosophy reduce all others to the masculine subject, the female disappears as a subject within discourse and thus only appears as the object. Although Irigaray proposes mimicry as a means to subvert the language, it would seem that any method that eradicates the self-representation of the masculine subject and allows the female to create herself as subject, as opposed to being a created object, would be permissible. To take the female body that had been "created" as the object, or as "art object" as Gubar states (Gubar 1985: 293), and rewrite it by transforming the text into body would enable the writer to escape the restrictions of traditional writing by placing the "masculine subject" on the female body and by subverting language by reverting to a presymbolic system of pictures and designs. There could be no monologic if the text is composed of images that can be aesthetic, referential, and symbolic all at the same time. Therefore, by writing/tattooing on the body, the woman creates a text that can be interpreted as representing her affinity for the aesthetic of the image, a personal relation to the image, a symbolic relation to the image, or possibly any number of other types of relation. The text is thus disruptive because it cannot be controlled. Without control it is difficult for the power structure to establish one's value in an economic system. This is different from cosmetics, in that tattooing posits any number of relationships between the individual and the image, while cosmetics generally posit one reading, that being the individual's relationship to the cultural aesthetic of beauty.

Tattooing, like many sign systems, by its very nature is dependent upon sight. Fredric Jameson, in a discussion on film, writes, "[t]he visual is *essentially* pornographic, which is to say that it has its end in rapt, mindless fascination" (Jameson 1990: 1). In fact, the tattooing of the female, if it is to accrue any subversive meaning and power, is dependent upon the pornographic aspect of the visual. Mary Ann Caws adds that the gaze "tends toward a certain violence, a will to penetrate, to pierce, to fix in order to discover the permanent under the changing appearances" (Caws 1985: 270). Since idealized, nude women have been the content of the visual arts since at least the Renaissance, they are what is accepted and expected; by mar(k)ing the body, the woman forces the male viewer to realize the difference between what he sees and what he is expected to see. The mar(k)ing of the body distances the woman from the cultural object that the masculine culture had created her to be; a space is created that forces the male viewer to reevaluate or reject her body. With this marked space, the female disrupts the masculine master-narrative of the visual; the gaze can no longer be stable in its domination because it can no longer be the same gaze. The object has shifted. "Given the heavy loading of cultural values, the media of irreversible body art are typically taken for granted by insiders and arouse strong (pre-dominantly negative) feelings among outsiders—usually fascination blended with distaste or even repugnance" (Rubin 1988: 16). Rubin points out that there is a great uncertainty in the response of the viewer; the traditional gaze explodes when it is forced to reconcile both fascin-ation and repugnance. The sensual allure of the exotic is juxtaposed on the rejection of his historic aesthetic. Does he stare, peek, or turn away? The tattooing of the female has forced the male to recognize his position as viewer; the text has the *potential* to recreate or revise the viewer's perceptions and expectations.

Tattooing, while it is a covering of the body, is also a revealing and affirming of the body and its sexuality. According to Roland Barthes, the striptease signifies "nakedness as a *natural* vesture of woman" (Barthes 1972: 85). The male gaze is epitomized in the striptease; the gaze is focused, anticipatory, and penetrative. It is the act of removing the veils that, according to Barthes, is the erotic and fascinating aspect of the striptease. Since the tattooed body cannot lose all its veilings, then the woman has succeeded in preventing the male viewer from the erotic anticipation of knowing that the veil can be removed; the tattoo becomes the covering that the viewer cannot take off. The body becomes part of the veil, which, depending on the extent to which a woman is tattooed, can cover the entire body. Irigaray proposes that the entire female body is potentially erogenous: "*woman has sex organs more or less every-where. She finds pleasure almost anywhere*" (Irigaray 1985a: 28). The tattoo, anywhere on the female body, then, can represent her veiled sexuality, denying and distancing the sexual intervention and penetration of the male gaze. The mar(k)ed body distances herself from the position of passive object; she now can control the text because it is part of her, but not part of the phallocentric discourse and exchange.

We have seen how the visual is indicted in creation of the woman-as-object dynamic; this can be extended so that writing itself is a positioning of the female in the space of the male gaze. In Angela Carter's discussion of the Marquis de Sade she states, "pornographic writing retains this in common with all literature—that it turns the flesh into word" (Carter 1978: 13). Not only is the female objectified, she is also reduced to the symbolic order, which is in itself an integral aspect of the patriarchal structure. Writing places the female body on the page for the reader to see. Just as the female body has been "admired" on the wall of the museum, so is it also on the page of the book. The sexual "object" body has been reduced to letters; in the process, however, the subject has not been allowed to return. The body in the book reflects the body on the wall. Via the medium of tattooing, the body is returned to its state as subject; the word becomes flesh. What had been reduced to letters and signifiers has been given body. By writing on the body, the author creates a interdependency between body and text; they are one. The viewer/reader cannot separate text from person because there is not a border.

Having the word become flesh parallels, mimics, and mocks the Christian order, which is responsible for much of the suppression of women anyway: "The Word became flesh and lived for a while among us" (John 1.14, *NIV*).

Another consequence of female tattooing is that it helps expose the constructed nature of the text, as well as suggesting that sexuality may also be a construction. Judith Butler writes "[t]here is no subject prior to its constructions, and neither is the subject determined by those constructions" (1993: 124). The subject results from constructions—it is created by a number of converging narratives, but does not have to be determined by them. Tattooing physically marks the body, and to that extent reveals the ease with which the body can be altered or "constructed." The tattoo is placed on the body and then becomes part of it; this parallels how culture imposes a narrative on the individual, who unwittingly assumes the narrative as his/her own. If, according to the society, a woman's sexuality is based on her appearance, then the alteration by tattooing of her appearance, of her body, alters the cultural construction of sexuality.

Any tattoo can be read as representative of the historic and violent imposition of the male narrative on the female body. Blanchard references Lévi-Strauss's idea that "writing is violent and . . . it hurts" (1994: 295). This doubles the violence of the tattoo; not only is the process violent but the text is violent as well. The actual process of tattooing in contemporary Western culture is not as violent as it is/was in less industrialized cultures and times; however, the act itself is the *penetration* into the female body by foreign objects, the needle and the metallic ink. Therefore the tattoo is a mark that signifies the penetration by the needle, and metaphorically by the patriarchal institutions of church, government, and family, as well as by the penis during the act of rape. The church, government, the family, business, and individual men have all imposed their separate narratives of control of the female body both physically and sexually, of silencing the female tongue, and of limiting the woman's possible roles within the society. The tattoo can act as the locus of memory, which, at any time, reveals the impositional nature of patriarchal institutions; each time the tattoo is seen, the penetration is recalled.

The pain inherent in tattooing has the potential to force the individual being tattooed into an increased consciousness of his/her self as well as his/her action. According to Gilles Deleuze in *Coldness and Cruelty*, "masochism gives primacy to the ego and to the process of idealization" (Deleuze 1991: 137). While one may argue that masochism and the pain received in tattooing are not similar, there does seem to be a common desire to experience pain and derive some pleasure from it. If, as Deleuze suggests, masochism gives primacy to the ego, then the pain inflicted during tattooing could likewise give primacy to the ego: the self of the person being tattooed would be central. For one who has been denied a self by the culture, tattooing could be a process that emphasizes the "self." James Scarborough, in an article for *Artweek*, claims that the process of getting a tattoo is as much a part of tattooing as the finished product (Scarborough 1992: 16). It would seem, thus, that the process is integral and cannot be separated from the tattoo itself. Deleuze adds that masochism functions to destroy the superego (Deleuze 1991: 130). By aiding in the destruction of the superego, masochism (pain) allows the individual to destroy the incorporated Law and other master-narratives to which the super-ego adheres. For one who is victim to those master-narratives, the pain of tattooing represents an opportunity to destroy the very part of the psyche that participates in those narratives. Finally, Deleuze argues that pain permits the individual to experience the pleasure forbidden by the law: "[t]he masochist regards the law as a punitive process and therefore begins by having the punishment inflicted upon himself; once he has undergone the punishment, he feels that he is allowed or indeed commanded to experience the pleasure that the law was supposed to forbid" (Deleuze 1991: 88). The physicality and sensuality of the body that have been forbidden for the female in patriarchal society are experienced in the act of being tattooed; she experiences her body.

For Western men, who have historically been the ones to impose master-narratives, being tattooed would seem to allow them little opportunity to experience the role of the marginalized. The tattoo represents the exoticism of the other, that "something" that he can never know because of his privileged position in the hierarchy. One could easily argue that the gay male shares many of the same impositions that the female has endured, and from that basis contend that he also might become tattooed for the same reasons as the female.

From Body on Canvas to Body as Canvas

The interpretations of the tattoo, or the representations of those females with them, that appear most prevalently are those of artist and outcast who has taken the tattoo as a means to get beyond the conventional objectification of the female body. Susan Gubar writes that the woman has been the object of art for ages, but not the creator: "Woman is not simply an object, however. If we think in terms of the production of culture, she is an art object: she is the ivory carving or mud replica, an icon or doll, but she is not the sculptor" (Gubar 1985: 293). Tattooing becomes the process of the woman creating and choosing her own text, whether or not she does the actual tattooing; she chooses how the body will appear. This potential distance from the woman/text and the inscriber of the text should not be dismissed by the creative communities, because artistic distance has been integral to the process or philosophy of many important male artists: Michelangelo and other Renaissance

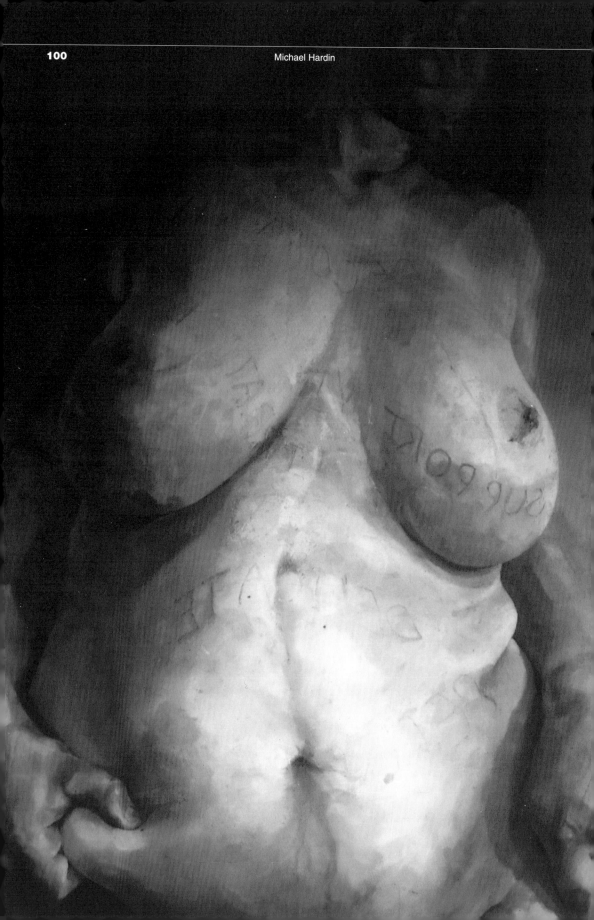

artists had apprentices fill in parts of their works; Marcel Duchamp would buy items at a hardware store and then present them as his ready-mades; Andy Warhol's silk screens were often created by persons in the Factory; and Robert Smithson's "Spiral Jetty" could only be made with the help of a crew of dump trucks. Also, the tattoo as sign of the artist can be read as the woman subverting/recreating the "artwork." Since women have been the objects of art for so long, by tattooing the body, the woman can take the object of the male artists, herself, and create her own text/self. Tattooing, then, is the process by which the female artist can take back what has been hers all along, her body. She transforms herself from the "perfect" reclining *Olympia* of Manet or the flattened *Les Demoiselles d'Avignon* of Picasso into who/whatever she chooses; she now controls the brush.

While little, if anything, has been written on the subject of contemporary female tattooing in the West, it has begun to appear as a significant motif in a number of contemporary texts and artworks by women.[6] The writer for whom the tattoo has the greatest textual significance is Kathy Acker. In an interview with Ellen Friedman, Acker says,

> [t]he most positive thing in the book [*Empire of the Senseless*] is the tattoo. It concerns taking over, doing your own sign-making . . . the tattoo is very much a sign of a certain class and certain people, a part of society that sees itself as outcast and shows it. For me tattooing is very profound. The meeting of body and . . . spirit—it's a *real* kind of art, it's on the skin . . . people . . . are beginning to take their own sign-making into their own hands. They're conscious of their own sign-making, signifying values really (Acker 1989: 17–18).

Tattooing allows her an association with the outcasts of society, and it is a means to take control, not only of one's signs, but also one's body. The tattoo and body join and become one; for Acker, it is also a meeting of body and spirit. In another passage, Acker describes how the tattoo is the primal parent of the visual arts and through time moves into the margins of societies:

Figure 3
Jenny Saville. "Branded."
213.5 × 183cm. Oil on canvas.
1992. Courtesy of The Saatchi
Gallery.

> The tattoo is primal parent of the visual arts. Beginning as abstract maps of spiritual visions, records of the "other" world, tattoos were originally icons of power and mystery designating realms beyond normal land-dwellers' experience . . . In decadent phases, the tattoo became associated with the criminal—literally the outlaw—and the power of the tattoo became intertwined with the power of those who chose to live beyond the norms of society (Acker 1988: 140).

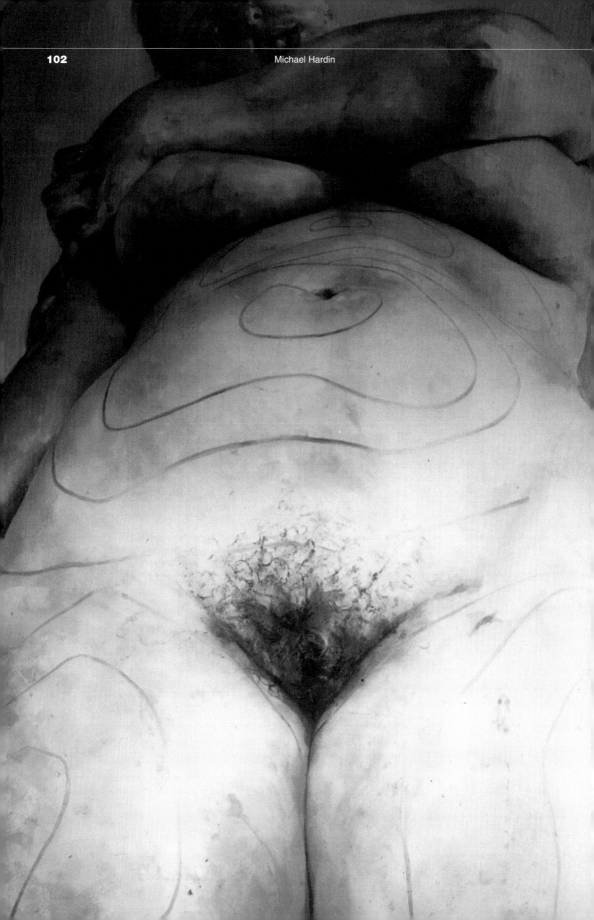

By placing tattooing at the origins of visual art, Acker is able to give it increased generative power, which she supplements with the power of the criminal, the outlaw, the outsider. For Acker, the tattoo is a way to exit the cultural and patriarchal exchange in which women serve as commodity and currency. To leave the exchange would bankrupt the institution; immense power is gained by the ability to leave.

The current work of the British artist Jenny Saville is also dependent upon the motif of inscribing the female body. She paints large, obese nude women with words inscribed into the paint of their flesh. In one, entitled *Branded*, words such as "decorative," "petite," and "supportive" are cut into/written onto her breasts, stomach, neck, and torso, marking her with the cultural identities imposed upon the female in society. In another, *Plan*, Saville has painted "contour lines . . . on her body to indicate the desired weight loss" (Kent 1994: 6). Saville comments on the beauty aesthetic in the West, namely Britain and the United States, and we can see her intent with these paintings through her critique of this aesthetic and the resulting consequences it has on women's perceptions of their own bodies:

> Nearly everyone I know . . . is obsessed with dieting—from anorectics who end up in hospital to friends who take hundreds of laxatives a day. It's like an epidemic. Tabloids like the *Daily Record* are full of information on how to improve your body and hide unsightly areas. Some American companies write the provision of body management into the contracts of female employees . . . What would beauty be, if everyone were the same? (cited by Kent 1994: 6).

The body, according to Saville, is the site of control; therefore she makes it the site of contest in her work. She challenges the viewer to such a degree that, in his review of the paintings for *Art in America*, Tony Godfrey makes a point of remarking that "viewers often backed away from them" (Godfrey 1994: 127). It seems quite obvious that the viewers backed away because they were confronted with a depiction of the female body that is not art-historically based; these are not the nudes of Titian, Rubens, Goya, or Manet, all of whom participated in the construction and maintenance of the ideal female body that Saville vehemently rejects. Another reason the viewer must step back is that there is no ambiguity regarding her agenda; she quite consciously inserts/inscribes her French feminist theory into her work—*Propped* has a large woman seated on a pedestal with the writing of Irigaray scratched into the surface of the paint.[7] Thus, when we read her work, we are reading her reading of the female body in Western culture in much the same way as we would read Barbara Kruger's work.[8]

Figure 4
Jenny Saville. "Plan." 274 × 213.5cm. Oil on canvas. 1993. Courtesy of The Saatchi Gallery.

Conclusion

The extensive presence of the motif of the woman as written text in contemporary feminism and women's writing forces one to make a complete revision of the role of woman in art and literature; no longer is she the object—she has taken control and written herself as the subject. The body, for centuries the site of control, has become the space for her voice. Cliff Raven, one of the leading tattoo artists, is paraphrased by Rubin as saying, "even in alienated, late Twentieth Century post-industrial society, the act of putting on a tattoo, as such, does not make a statement about the system, nor does it constitute a revolutionary act" (Rubin 1988: 225). Then why is this phenomenon appearing among so many different women: lesbians, women of color, heterosexual women, Anglos? Consciously or not, the woman as text becomes an image that enables the woman to place herself as reactionary to the imposition of the patriarchal narrative: the tattoo confronts the historic penetration of the male text, denies men the visual pleasure of the female object, and allows for a new space that expands the potential for female creativity, authority, and subjectivity. By being both subject and text, the woman can control her space in the narrative and arrange events so that she can now create her own significance; meaning is still created, but now the woman can create a self outside of the male exchange. Her identity is no longer dependent upon her commodification but upon her self-narration.

Notes

1. This is not even to mention the current debate in the United States over abortion and a woman's control of her own body.
2. In the analysis by Teilhet-Fisk, there is no indication whether or not the beauty aesthetic is imposed by the males or the females within the culture.
3. Even though liposuction and breast implants are also permanent, they function within the patriarchal ideology of beauty because they do not mar the object but "enhance" it.
4. In "The Body Eclectic" (*Downtown Voice* [Houston] 1.6 [1994]: 16–19), Christine Adams reports that numerous tattoo parlors tell her that women constitute more of their clientele percentage than men do. This observation fits with my own observations that a greater number of my female acquaintances have tattoos than do my male acquaintances.
5. An example of women taking a negative image and giving it new significance are the Chicana and Mexicana critics and theorists who have recently been demythifying la Malinche (Doña Marina,

Figure 5
Jenny Saville. "Propped."
213.5 × 183cm. Oil on canvas.
1992. Courtesy of The Saatchi
Gallery.

Malintzin), one of the most hated women in Mexican lore, and have redefined her as an example of a powerful, intelligent, and creative female.

6. In Emily Prager's novel, *Eve's Tattoo* (New York: Random, 1991), the tattoo is the medium through which the protagonist, Eve Flick, can identify with those disenfranchised women of Second World War Germany who ended up in the concentration camps.

In *The Woman Warrior: Memoirs of a Childhood Among Ghosts* (New York: Vintage, 1989), by Maxine Hong Kingston, the image is more clearly defined. For the woman warrior, the tattoo is inscribed by the parents and becomes a source of power: "'We are going to carve revenge on your back . . . We'll write out oaths and names' . . . 'I saw my back covered entirely with words in red and black files, like an army, like my army'" (Kingston 1989: 34–35).

Elizabeth McCracken, in the opening story "It's Bad Luck to Die" of *Here's Your Hat What Your Hurry* (New York: Turtle Bay, 1993), uses tattooing as a motif that expresses the woman's individual self and body but also represents the relation of the female to the male and the patriarchal gaze.

Written on the Body (New York: Knopf, 1993), by Jeanette Winterson, does not deal with tattooing as such, but, as the title indicates, the work focuses on the body as text. In the novel, what is read is the desire for the lover of the narrator on the narrator's body: "When I try to read, it's you I'm reading" (Winterson 1993: 15); "This is the body where your name is written, passing into the hands of strangers" (1993: 178). The marking of the body is a sign of love and devotion, a memory of past encounters.

The tattooed female body has also appeared as an illustration for the covers and frontispieces of various anthologies of women's writing. On the cover of *Chicana Lesbians: The Girls Our Mothers Warned Us About*, edited by Carla Trujillo (Berkeley, CA: Third Woman Press, 1991) is la Virgen de Guadalupe tattooed on the back of a woman. Corinna Sargood has illustrated Angela Carter's two collections of fairy tales, both of which have the backs of tattooed female torsos on the frontispieces. On the frontispiece of *Strange Things Sometimes Still Happen: Fairy Tales from Around the World* (Boston: Faber and Faber, 1993) is a tattooed back with intricate floral designs, interspersed with animals, Adam and Eve holding apples, and a skeletal grim reaper. The frontispiece to *The Old Wives' Fairy Tale Book* (New York: Pantheon, 1990) displays the back of a woman on whom are drawn a winged mermaid queen, animals, birds, and dragons. On each of these three pictures is a mythic narrative; the female body, specifically and symbolically the back, becomes the text for the transference of cultural capital. It is the role of the female in these mythic narratives that the female must subvert or challenge through incorporation: as la Virgen, the woman is removed from sexuality and her individual existence—she has identity only through her role as mother to Christ; the mermaid is the woman who attempts to seduce Odysseus and other sailors to their deaths through sexuality and sensual songs; Eve is the woman who is blamed for the fall of all *man*kind. By placing these myths on the female body, the woman can take the representation and change the context, effectively, or at least potentially, changing the myth.

7. "If we continue to speak in this sameness, speak as men have spoken for centuries, we will fail each other again."

8. A good example of Kruger's work that does the same thing as Saville's is "Your gaze hits the side of my face," a 1981 work that has those words over a picture of a profiled marble head of a woman.

References

Acker, Kathy. 1988. *Empire of the Senseless*. New York: Grove.

———. 1989. "A Conversation with Kathy Acker" (interviewed by Ellen G. Friedman). *The Review of Contemporary Fiction* 9(3): 12–22.

Barthes, Roland. 1922. *Mythologies*, trans. Annette Lavers. New York: Noonday.

Blanchard, Marc. 1994. "Post-Bourgeois Tattoo: Reflections on Skin Writing in Late Capitalist Societies." In *Visualizing Theory: Selected Essays from* Visual Anthropology Review 1990–1994, ed. Lucien Taylor, pp. 287–300. New York: Routledge.

Butler, Judith. 1993. *Bodies That Matter: On the Discursive Limits of "Sex."* London: Routledge.

Carter, Angela. 1978. *The Sadeian Woman: And the Ideology of Pornography*. New York: Pantheon.

Caws, Mary Ann. 1985. "Ladies Shot and Painted: Female Embodiment in Surrealist Art." In *The Female Body in Western Culture*, ed. Susan Rubin Suleiman, pp. 262–87. Cambridge, MA: Harvard University Press.

Deleuze, Gilles. 1991. *Coldness and Cruelty*. In *Masochism:* Coldness and Cruelty *by Gilles Deleuze and* Venus in Furs *by Leopold von Sacher-Masoch*, pp. 1–138. New York: Zone Books.

Foucault, Michel. 1990. *The History of Sexuality: Volume I: An Introduction*, trans. Robert Hurley. New York: Vintage.

Godfrey, Tony. 1994. "Jenny Saville at the Saatchi Collection." *Art in America* 82(5): 127.

Gotch, Christopher and Ronald Scutt. 1974. *Skin Deep: The Mystery of Tattooing*. London: Peter Davies.

Gubar, Susan. 1985. "'The Blank Page' and the Issues of Female Creativity." In *The New Feminist Criticism: Essays on Women, Literature, and Theory*, ed. Elaine Showalter, pp. 292–313. New York: Pantheon.

Hambly, W. D. 1925. *The History of Tattooing and Its Significance: With Some Account of Other Forms of Corporal Marking*. London: H. F. & G. Witherby.

Irigaray, Luce. 1985a. *This Sex Which Is Not One*, trans. Catherine Porter. Ithaca, NY: Cornell University Press.

——. 1985b. *Speculum of the Other Woman*, trans. Gillian C. Gill. Ithaca, NY: Cornell University Press.

Jameson, Fredric. 1990. *Signatures of the Visible*. London: Routledge.

Kent, Sarah. 1994. "Young British Artists III: Simon Callery, Simon English, Jenny Saville: The Saatchi Gallery." London: Saatchi Gallery.

Lévi-Strauss, Claude. 1963. *Structural Anthropology*, trans. Claire Jacobson and Brooke Grundfest Schoepf. New York: Basic.

Marcus, Jane. 1991. "Laughing at Leviticus: *Nightwood* as Woman's Circus Epic." In *Silence and Power: A Reevaluation of Djuna Barnes*, ed. Mary-Lynn Broe, pp. 221–50, 397–400. Carbondale, IL: Southern Illinois University Press.

Rubin, Arnold. 1988. *Marks of Civilization: Artistic Transformations of the Human Body*, ed. Arnold Rubin. Los Angeles: Museum of Cultural History, University of California Los Angeles.

Sanders, Clinton R. 1989. "Organizational Constraints on Tattoo Images: A Sociological Analysis of Artistic Style." In *The Meanings of Things: Material Culture and Symbolic Expression*, ed. Ian Hodder, pp. 232–41. London: Unwin Hyman.

Scarborough, James. 1992. "Illustrative Bodies: *Forever Yes: Art of the New Tattoo* at Bryce Banna Tyne Gallery." *Artweek* 23 16–17.

Showalter, Elaine. 1990. *Sexual Anarchy: Gender and Culture at the Fin de Siecle*. New York: Viking.

Steward, Samuel M. 1990. *Bad Boys and Tough Tattoos: A Social History of the Tattoo with Gangs, Sailors and Street-Corner Punks, 1950–1965*. New York: Harrington Park Press.

Suleiman, Susan Rubin. 1985. "(Re)Writing the Body: The Politics and Poetics of Female Eroticism." In ed. S. R. Suleiman, pp. 7–29. Cambridge, MA: Harvard University Press.

Teilhet-Fisk, Jehanne. 1988. "The Spiritual Significance of Newar Tattoos." In *Marks of Civilization: Artistic Transformations of the Human Body*, ed. Rubin, pp. 135–40. Los Angeles: Museum of Cultural History, University of California Los Angeles.

Thévoz, Michel. 1985. *The Painted Body: The Illusions of Reality*. New York: Rizzoli.

Weideger, Paula. 1986. *History's Mistress: A New Interpretation of a Nineteenth-Century Classic*. New York: Viking Penguin.

Winterson, Jeanette, 1993. *Written on the Body*. New York: Knopf.

Fashion Theory, Volume 3, Issue 1, pp.109–120
Reprints available directly from the Publishers.
Photocopying permitted by licence only.
© 1999 Berg. Printed in the United Kingdom.

A Note:
Art & Fashion,
Viktor & Rolf

Richard Martin

Richard Martin, Curator of The
Costume Institute of The
Metropolitan Museum of Art, is
Adjunct Professor of Art History
and Archaeology at Columbia
University and Adjunct Professor of
Art at New York University. From
1974–1988 he was Editor of *Arts
Magazine*, and for twenty years he
taught art history at the Fashion
Institute of Technology where he
also served as Executive Director
of the Shirley Goodman Resource
Center and Executive Director of
the Educational Foundation for the
Fashion Industries.

Three years ago, The 1996 Biennale of Fashion in Florence juxtaposed
art and fashion to a result that was little surprise. Art appealed for
fashion's corporeal expertise and metaphor; fashion yearned under these
circumstances for art's awe. Whether these were sibling rivalries intrinsic
to these arts or merely the suppositions of ambitious curators, the effect
was ultimately not to reconcile art and fashion, but to sunder them ever
more, tainting art with ostensible commerce and ephemerality and cast-
ing fashion in the role of obsequious courtier to art's long-lost *gravitas*.

Viktor & Rolf, the brilliant Dutch conceptualists, have always tried
to put art and fashion back together. If their task only seems to get harder,
so, too, their efforts become more refined. They remain inexorably

idealist about the nexus between art and fashion; they do not assume the bifurcated world, but choose to function on the axiom that art and fashion are similar if not identical impulses. The candor, criticality, and originality of their work begin in a principle of synthesis and harmony. On seeing their work, seldom does the spectator inquire as to whether the work is art or fashion, as likewise the Wagner watcher/listener will not ask if it is music or theater. The underlying principle of consonance among the visual arts is evident in the work of Viktor & Rolf. In their pursuit in concept and in practice, this creative team makes us believe, as they do, in an art without embarrassing hierarchies or demeaning classifications, but filled with contemporary visuality.

The collaboration, since 1993, is even more a hybrid of creativity and criticality than it is of art and fashion. Viktor & Rolf evince indomitable optimism. Artists such as Victor Burgin, Sylvie Fleury, and Judith Shea have sought to reproach fashion for its oppressions. In freeing themselves of the hierarchy, Viktor & Rolf have also freed themselves from fashion's meanest puritanical guilt, a penitence that might also deny us all the pleasures of painting and sculpture if Savonarola had prevailed. Describing their work as "experiments," Viktor & Rolf affect a rational and scientific objectivity even to the consumerism that surrounds fashion. For example, *Viktor & Rolf, le parfum* (1996) provides—except for the notable lack of scent—an elegant and wholly plausible fragrance bottle packaged with the finesse and inculcation of desire of modern marketing and the accompanying elements of promotion, including slick, desiring photography, an advertising campaign, and a press release. Viktor & Rolf deceive us in the absence of scent, but they are fundamentally honest. They know that advertising allure is readily simulated and images easily manipulated; they know that a commerce exists in "evanescence" and a seduction "more appealing than the answer." It is most refreshing that Viktor & Rolf do not show a distant, lofty haughtiness about things and especially about fashion. Art, which is also bought and sold and exists within a highly privileged and rarefied milieu, has been known to disdain fashion, but Viktor & Rolf seize fashion with the same kind of unabashed enthusiasm we associate with the generation of artists of the 1950s and 1960s who appropriated popular culture and its vivid imagery into Pop Art. Anthropologically, we never should have expected to leave the 1990s without a reckoning with the powerful and ubiquitous advertising for that intangible, but yearned for, commodity of fragrance. Creatively, we are only fulfilled when the banal beauty of fragrance advertising is given artistic reflection by artists such as Viktor & Rolf.

Another brilliant, if more modest, production by Viktor & Rolf is their numbered, limited-edition (2,500) plastic shopping bag. Not only does a concept make fashion and art coincide in this gesture, but there is also in this uncomplicated work a purity and simplicity characteristic of Viktor & Rolf.

Figure 1
Viktor & Rolf Couture.
Autumn/Winter 1999.
Courtesy of 2ᵉ Bureau.

Similarly, the recent installation *Launch* (1996) at Torch Gallery, Amsterdam identifies Viktor & Rolf's identification with the full spectrum of fashion. The artists aver of the installation, "For one instant, we create a dreamy situation where everything is forced to our will." In witnessing this white-cube installation, we know that art and fashion share the ideal of the "dreamy," controlled, and perfected world. Art no less than fashion, certainly in such examples as the deliberate installations of Russian Constructivism or the modern design of twentieth-century abstraction and its receiving-rooms in galleries and museums, demands the pure space of dreaming. Viktor & Rolf set up a sequence of fashion's system, including a runway or catwalk, sketching and draping session, and a photo shoot with seamless paper behind. In this clarified space, Viktor & Rolf presented the process of fashion, all parts familiar, but the whole seldom seen in an art gallery. But the artists achieve not the process, but the visible integrity of fashion, its comprehensive vision as a creative endeavor. The elements that we see unfold over time, from the design of the dress to its presentation on the runway, are here condensed into one moment, and fashion becomes a distilled and powerful image. Typically of Viktor & Rolf, the condensation of all the elements of fashion into one place makes them both more critical and more glamorous. In no way are fashion's aura and magnetism diminished. On the contrary, this installation demonstrates fashion's power, its transcendence, its presence to be "art" in the awesome sense and "art" in the common sense of late twentieth-century culture.

The mechanism of fashion has been part of Viktor & Rolf's work since their first collection, shown at the Salon Européen des Jeunes Stylistes (1993). To present art as a collection, as opposed to the high-bred supposition of individual works of art, is immediately to accept a contemporary convention for our seeing. Culturally, we want to see thematically, and often in terms larger than one. Viktor & Rolf used pre-existing fragments as the collage medium to create new clothing. Referring, of course, to the prevailing interest in deconstruction in fashion and the visual arts in 1993, Viktor & Rolf insisted in their intermediate world between art and fashion on the collage aspect of their work. The effect is to see, as in early Picasso collages, a new order emerging from the familiar pieces of old style. Fashion, which has in modern times avoided the distressed or the recycled, reverted to its own tradition in being ready to accommodate pastiche and its accompanying senses of memory and ambiguity.

Viktor & Rolf's *Collection #2* (1994, for Fall–Winter 1994–95) made of Malevich's experimentation a modiste's exercise. Viktor & Rolf offered a suite of variations on a white dress, accepting fashion as a site of infinite variations and permutations. Viktor & Rolf's virtuoso transfigurations of the white dress varied from high-waisted gowns that might have been ivory ballgowns for an *ancien régime* court, to others that seemed more like the amorphous forms of Comme des Garçons dresses.

Figure 2
Viktor & Rolf Couture.
Autumn/Winter 1999.
Courtesy of 2ᵉ Bureau.

Collection #3 (1994, for Summer 1995) focused on the theme of radical modernism. The *Black Square Dress* (1994) from the Collection squares off the shoulders to create an abstraction, but one that is always modified by the presence of the model who wears the clothing. Abstraction's presence is evident in this and in the earlier collection; but Viktor & Rolf's insistent referencing to the human body and to the fashion presentation makes the abstraction seem more humane and less intransigent. The collections have continued, most recently with *Collection #7* (1996, for Summer 1997), a series of compositions softer and more curvilinear than before in wrapping the body with a transmutable white dress worn over a gray bodysuit. *Winter of Love* (1994), presented at the Musée d'Art Moderne de la ville de Paris and later at P.S.1, the avant-garde performance space in New York, began a series of reflective *doppelgängers* for Viktor & Rolf. Wondrous white dresses could seem to have stepped out of a Second Empire ballroom, but they come ghost-like into our contemporary gallery setting or, in New York, an installation including gold garment templates as well.

Other fashion manifestations include the winter 1995–96 *Prêt-à-Porter Catalogue* (1995), a series of blue PVC modules in pants and bodysuits accompanied with white cotton, silk organza, and black wool jackets. The effect is both robotic and hypnotic, offering basic modules in complicated variations. Other works have been presented both as collections and as a gallery installation.

Collection #5: L'apparence du Vide (1995) was presented at Galerie Patricia Dorfmann in Paris. Five suspended gold garments of several different silhouettes might have initially seemed to be a marionette homage to the rich and ostentatious. But Viktor & Rolf never offer fashion as a mere convention. Instead, they interpret and involve the fashion that we might otherwise take to be superficial. One wall surrounding the clothing types was printed in gold letters with the MTV-familiar names of top contemporary "super-models." A sound system played the models' names spoken in repeated incantation in the voices of young girls. In the middle of this mantra of celebrity super-models and their adulation, the glittering gold of these mannequin-surrogates was haunting, but even more so the shadows they cast on the gallery floor. Viktor & Rolf created black "shadow-silhouettes" to articulate the floor of the gallery. Though prone and in that state wholly flat, the shadow pieces were each capable of being worn independently. These more sinister *doppelgängers* to the shining effigies remind us of fashion's essence in silhouette and life's counterpart in the shadow of mortality. Shadows remind us of the sun and of mortality; Viktor & Rolf give fashion both stories, illumination and transience.

Sweet indulgence, fashion's accustomed image, is invariably complemented by Viktor & Rolf's shadows and metaphorical shadows. Their *Shadowdress* (1995) is the living, three-dimensional form of what had appeared on the floor in *Collection #5*. This dark, translucent dress is in the nature of fashion's transparency and works as a viable fashion postulation. Yet it is also for Viktor & Rolf a component of their vacillation between feasible fashion and narrative, judgmental art. Likewise, *Shadow (Cape)* (1996) assumes the powerful silhouette of an 1890s torso, but in fragile silk organza, a figment of one *fin-de-siècle* that appears at the next *fin-de-siècle*. If this garment is in any way a shroud and yet wholly in the realm of fashion visualization, it should be a sign that fashion can be complex and configured.

Both art and fashion have been inimical to sustained cooperation. In a century in which some of the best ideas have happened in instances of collaboration between Salvador Dali and Schiaparelli and Christian Dior and Yves Saint Laurent, both arts continue to feel powered by the model of the singular, isolated romantic artist. Dolce & Gabbana and Badgely–Mischka remain anomalous as fashion pairs. Gilbert & George and McDermott & McGough are equally unusual as art collaborators. Two artists of a single identity defy our conventions of artistic authority just as much as they mock facile expectations about the twins of fashion and art.

Art critic Olivier Zahm plays the partisan when in the December 1995 issue of *Artforum* (New York) he declares Viktor & Rolf the "best" in style in 1995, and proclaims: "their fashion, or better 'metafashion,' amounts to a conceptual exercise in 'reconstruction.' As such, it is a stunning commentary on the ostentatious ambitions of fashion, involving an impassioned quest for novelty even as it acknowledges the radical impossibility of this undertaking." But is not the work of Viktor & Rolf as much a "meta-art" as a "meta-fashion?" The hybrid of art and fashion that Viktor & Rolf so distinctively—so uniquely—make cannot be measured against art or fashion alone, but must be measured against something larger and more important than either privileged discourse or outreach to the rich and elect. In refusing to accept the putative conceptual detachment of art or the supposed superficiality of fashion, Viktor & Rolf offer us a product of consumption and delectation, concept and contemplation. If we cannot narrowly call the work of Viktor & Rolf either "art" or "fashion," then we have an exciting challenge. We must see our visual culture with innocent freshness and without categories or hierarchy, as Viktor & Rolf do.

To wit, Viktor & Rolf presented a spring–summer 1998 couture collection wholly in the context of the couture showings in Paris. *The New York Times* and other journalists attended the collection on 21 January 1998 shown in the Taddeus Roppac Gallery. Even though it was not an officially sanctioned event of the Fédération de la Couture with its accustomed rules and waiting-periods for admission, Viktor & Rolf's collection was reviewed by *Le Figaro*, *Le Monde*, and other journals. This collection sustains Viktor & Rolf's taxonomy of art for fashion production and fashion for artmaking, identifying the ingredients and then adding the creativity that constitutes couture. To

skeptics, the couture is an atrophying and money-losing system that maintains only a few traditions of craft and a superannuated prestige. To the *cognoscenti*, couture is more than ever the workshop and display system of the boldest, most uninhibited by economics, purest system for fashion ideas and ambitions.

In Stephen Gan's *Visionaire 2000* (1997), Viktor & Rolf are characterized as "fashion's biggest fans and its toughest critics." The critical appreciation they evince is indicative of the intellectual and emotional tightrope they dance between art and fashion. The former discipline is ready with its canon and cornucopia of criticism and almost too eager to pronounce judgment at length. The latter discipline is more often thought to be incapable of assessing tough values or permitting reproach. Shrewdly, Viktor & Rolf found another art–fashion fusion and played with it in this performance: a sound track repeated the artists' names over and over again to the point of the mantric or the maniacal.

Viktor & Rolf's 1998 runway presentation mingled statue and runway, letting us see both the living statue of a fine-arts identity and the animation of a couture showing. The models walked out into the room as on a runway, but actually mounted a pedestal. In an analytical system of 25 dresses, the audacious artist-designers splayed out the process and evolution of garments and their concepts. Cautiously, they began with technique, studies from the toile, reminding us not only of the atelier toiles, but even of the canvas on which painting begins. To fundamental technique, they added form, chiefly the historical silhouettes (and the black material, beginning with the fourth man-nequin, equals the silhouette) as identified with white crumpled fabric—pseudo-crinolines and dry-cleaning stuffings underneath—as con-struction to render them vaguely archaic. Silhouette, often ignored in the streamlining of modern fashion, even couture, was remembered by Viktor & Rolf as a clothing option, though clearly not a necessity, or as they describe it "very beautiful, but in our time empty and meaningless."

To technique and form, Viktor & Rolf (and every other designer) added the elements, treatments for sleeves, collars, and the familiar signifiers for a garment. Here, the recipe for making clothing was revealed, but these designers know that this is no mere index, but the adjudication of elements. Therefore, the signifying elements of dress for Viktor & Rolf can be redisposed, in the para-Surrealist manner of misaligning a bodice and a sleeve, a conundrum between pants and dress, and the ambiguities of a dress and separates. They know well what Hubert de Givenchy perfected in the 1950s: his sweet, but Schiaparelli-inspired and Dior-aware, "split-levels" that seemed impossible to discern between a dress and a two-piece skirt and bodice.

Likewise, color is not intractable or fixed for Viktor & Rolf. What reads from one view as white may be yellow from another. They know and demonstrated on a black-blue tuxedo that color is fugitive and complicated, not just a crayon box. The excitement of color resides in

Figure 3
Viktor & Rolf Couture.
Courtesy of 2ᵉ Bureau.

the delicate, fracturing instability of the kaleidoscope, not in a list of tints. One remembers the midnight-blue formalwear of the Duke of Windsor: he chose blue instead of black to allow the black-and-white photographers a crisper image in black. Thus, he achieved black through the mis-impression of a blue tuxedo. Likewise, Viktor & Rolf addressed fabrics and their strong sense of designer identity, choosing specific identifiers for Liberty and Yves Saint Laurent, but recognizing that fabric implies and involves more than material; it engages the identity and even the name of the designer. Similarly, the stripes and dots and checks that are a vocabulary of textile constitute a structure and strategy in clothing as much as Daniel Buren's stripes in art.

Viktor & Rolf simulated the accretions of *les petites mains*, especially embroidery, that exceptional and unequalled capacity of the couture to sparkle, to tell a story, and to impart glamor. A gray dress (#20) is embroidery in process: sequins and beads are just emerging from their pinned gold/silver/black balls. This is not the end-result embroidery of Lesage, but the chrysalis of embroidery (and as Viktor & Rolf point out, more like a hobby embroidery than debonair professional embroidery), the fantasies that embroidery can confer captured at inception just before glamor happens, just before the decorative system emerges, just before the hard sequins surrender to the pliant form of the dress.

Viktor & Rolf understand the provisional aspect of couture's hats and necklaces. These are supporting players to the primary drama of the dress: the couture has understood that its clients can see designer jewelry, even more ephemeral than costume jewelry, with desired garments because they possess the real jewelry to wear with dresses of distinction. Who really needs these accessories in the world of the couture? In Viktor & Rolf's couture show, these accessories, while added into the index and list of ingredients, ended up being superfluous.

Thus, the index is complex. Analytically and intellectually, the constituents of couture have been summoned and summed up: **technique, form, dress elements, color, fabric, pattern, embroidery,** and **accessories.** The chef knows the recipe; we have defined the parts that build the couture. Viktor & Rolf offered a studious and creative summation, letting the taxonomy speak. It is perhaps not to ruin the end of the story to say that she is not couture's accustomed and romantic bride, but a creature of utter chaos, the many components coming together in confusion and uncertainty. Her final deception was to smash her massive necklace and ceramic hat, requiring spectators to realize that what they assumed was soft and fashionable was, in fact, hard and deceitful. As both critics and creators, intellectuals and artisans, Viktor & Rolf rendered into abstract principles the components and composition of the couture. As fashion designers, committed to the singular garment and to experimentation in clothing that can be worn, Viktor & Rolf reminded us that the couture cannot be reduced to a set of precepts or system and that its mere index

Figure 4
Viktor & Rolf Couture.
Courtesy of 2ᵉ Bureau.

is insufficient. The concluding and comprehensive element is the creative and magical, the transubstantiation from an inventory of elements to the commanding vision of the couture.

In the 1990s (and, in fact, ever since the 1960s), many cynics have questioned the couture and many have reported that it is a weak and waning institution. Some say only those with a vested commercial interest in the couture advocate its continuance and future. Then, suddenly a brilliant and provocative pair of artist-designers with no such vested interest in the couture make us realize, chiefly on the model of art theory and art producing, that couture is that more-than-the-sum-of-its-parts practice. Visual theory and scientific reasoning provide a taxonomy, all the constituents, but only Art, the infinitely unaccountable and the wonderful, renders the couture. Could fashion alone have offered us a runway both viable and critical? Perhaps, inasmuch as Rei Kawakubo for Comme des Garçons or Martin Margiela have both recognized the runway's dilation into conceptualism. Could art without fashion have offered the same lesson? Perhaps, but art's instruction is so often rarefied and so rarely exact. Instead, Viktor & Rolf have purposely taken us to that ambiguous place where we are not sure if it is art or fashion that is speaking; but the message is that art and fashion can be involved and even be indivisible. Did any garments from this collection sell? Rarely would the couture tell; seldom would art reveal; little should we want to know; for, somehow or other, this is high art and/or high fashion.

Fashion Theory, Volume 3, Issue 1, pp.121–126
Reprints available directly from the Publishers.
Photocopying permitted by licence only.

Exhibition Review: *Addressing the Century: 100 Years of Art & Fashion.* The Hayward Gallery

**Reviewed by
Clare Coulson**

October 8 –
January 11, 1999

At a time of unprecedented correlation between the visual arts and design, *Addressing the Century: 100 Years of Art & Fashion* at the Hayward Gallery, London takes a look back at the moments when art and fashion have met during the past 100 years. Following the 1996 Biennale and the Guggenheim's Art/Fashion in 1997, curators Peter Wollen and Fiona Bradley hope to elucidate this complex exchange of ideas.

While fashion and art have always enjoyed a fruitful relationship, the boundaries between the two have become increasingly blurred during this century. The exhibits, taken from across the spectrum of visual arts from 1910 to the present day, are divided into five sections: Decoration, Function, Fantasy, Performance and Convergence.

Traditional hierarchies in the arts, with fine art at the top and dress (as an artisan/craft-based activity) at the very bottom, have been consistently challenged this century. Artists have drawn upon fashion, elevating its status, while fashion has questioned its own ephemerality and now graces the gallery as well as the department store.

Addressing the Century opens with the arts and crafts revival that included the Wiener Werkstätte in Vienna and the Omega workshops in London. In an attempt to combine practicality with contemporary decoration, this movement nurtured the fusion between art and fashion. Gustav Klimt applied his opulent designs to dress while Poiret developed couture by pursuing his own interest in artistic dress; he used fabric from the Wiener Werkstätte and collaborated with contemporary Fauve painters. Matisse's sumptuous Mandarin costume for "Le Chant du Rossignol," 1920, illustrates these relationships and the orientalism that echoed throughout the period, especially in the designs for Sergei Diaghilev's *Ballets Russes*.

Zaha Hadid's exhibition design changes radically in each section. Here, pieces are laid out flat in low display cases. While this allows close inspection of fabrics it does not work well in a busy space. When exhibition design is installed at the cost of the visitor's experience, one wonders what the show's creators are trying to achieve.

Opulent decoration gives way to function and modernity in the 1920s when the Futurists and Russian Constructivists worked towards creating dress for the masses inspired by their total art aesthetic. Their revolutionary ideas were fuelled by radical politics: the Futurists issued Balla's Manifesto of Dress in 1914. The Function section is disappointingly disjointed with Sonia Delaunay's work in closer proximity to the Surrealists than to the Futurists, with whom she surely had more in common. Oskar Schlemmer's 1922 figurines from *The Triadic Ballet* are stunning but in Hadid's design they were isolated from other sections. As with the exhibition as a whole, there was no ongoing theoretical discourse. Themes could have been explored throughout the sections and this would undoubtedly have clarified the extremely complex issues. The lack of theoretical underpinning in this exhibition is surprising when there are numerous themes to be explored. Perhaps it is assumed that the catalogue will clarify these themes yet even here the list of works is not presented in the most user-friendly manner.

Function had little to do with Surrealist fashion. Dali's Aphrodisiac Dinner Jacket of 1934 illustrates why this was not a period in which fashion fused with art in the way it previously had. The drawings of Elsa Schiaparelli and Salvador Dalí reflect how closely they worked creating fantastical, bizarre designs with accessories as a focal point.

The 1960s, a decade of great political, social and economic change, saw art and fashion move closer together than ever before and, for the first time, these changes took place at all levels of fashion. Once more, divisions were blurred by Pop and Op art and ground-breaking designers

Figure 1
Comme des Garçons,
Spring/Summer 1997
Collection.

such as Courrèges and Paco Rabanne redefined their roles. New materials such as plastic and paper were used to create barely-there shifts while Lucio Fontana moved from art to couture. His metallic paper dress of 1961 echoed his slashed canvases. Performance defines the period as art objects "acquire the paradoxical status of existing both as wearable clothes, crafted for their own creators, and as aesthetic icons with a conceptual life of their own."

Fashion photography was central to these changes and is represented well in the exhibition. F. C. Gundlach's striking *OP-Art Fashion* of 1966 chronicles these new movements in art and fashion. The impact of fashion photographers has continued to this day; influential photographers such as Deborah Turberville and Nick Knight are included and illustrate how the arts have become fused in the 1980s and 1990s. Equally at home in the gallery as in a glossy magazine, contemporary photographers have undoubtedly contributed to the evolving relationship between art and fashion.

Nick Knight has consistently challenged preconceived ideas about fashion and beauty over the past two decades and is given just prominence at *Addressing the Century*. His 1986 picture of a Yohji Yamamoto coat seems more concerned with creating an object of beauty than with the detail of the garment.

Today distinctions between the visual arts and fashion appears more blurred than ever before. The exhibition's final section, Convergence, is visually and conceptually innovative and could have formed the basis for an entire exhibition.

In this final section the suspension of garments in mid-air is an inspired method of display; sculptural pieces including those by Issey Miyake, Deborah Milner and Roberto Capucci slowly rotated allowing visitors to see the whole garment and to experience the way in which these clothes metamorphose. Rei Kawakubo's innovative and distorted gingham pieces are displayed alongside Cindy Sherman's advertising campaigns for Comme des Garçons and runway footage. Her total art aesthetic is cleverly interpreted within the gallery space. Avant-garde, sculptural and revolutionary, these pieces are often seen in an art context and this is in many cases a conscious development—collaborations with artists are surely intended to expand the meaning of a garment.

These designers consciously resist categorization. They want their work to exist where form and function are harmoniously fused and ideas flow freely. Their work is both art and fashion. It is in this final section that art seems most closely linked to fashion. Adrian Bannon's Thistledown Coat of 1998 reflects our contemporary obsession with identity and transience—discourses that are inextricably linked to dress and the presentation of the self.

A new arts and crafts spirit has given rise to a generation of designers who constantly seek to avoid the classification of dress-maker and elevate their designs to art forms. Conversely, contemporary artists seldom confine themselves to working on canvas and frequently turn to fabrics and fashion as a mode of expression. Traditional hierarchies in the Arts are rapidly evaporating as fashion design has become as much to do with biannual performance as it is concerned with form and function.

The exhibition documents not only the fusions and diffusions of ideas and inspirations in art and fashion but also the development of cultural identity. Contemporary designers such as Hussein Chalayan and Martin Margiela baffle the fashion press with their collections, presented as performance. Increasingly their work is perceived as being cerebral and more akin to art than the commerce-driven world of high fashion. It is timely then that the exhibition addresses this very theme. Despite the apparent lack of methodology, *Addressing the Century* offers a timely re-examination of one of fashion's most enduring themes and tackles complex issues with a refreshingly novel approach.

Fashion Theory, Volume 3, Issue 1, pp.127–130
Reprints available directly from the Publishers.
Photocopying permitted by licence only.

Exhibition Review:
Seeing + hearing
= dressing

Reviewed by
Patrizia Calefato

December 5, 1997 –
March 3, 1998

"Shut your eyes and feel the music. Listen to it and see the garments that have heralded in fashions." These sentences welcome visitors to the exhibition *Vedere + sentire = vestire* (*Seeing + hearing = dressing*), which ran from December 5th 1997 to March 3rd 1998 at the Vintage Palace A.N.G.E.L.O. in Lugo di Romagna (Ravenna, Italy). The Palace is a three-storey building housing used clothing that was inaugurated in 1992 by Angelo Caroli and Mario Gulmanelli. Inside there are over 50,000 used garments, all selected, subdivided and cleaned, and a few thousand accessories. This is a true historical archive of Vintage fashions from various periods, collected from every part of the globe and exhibited in a unique permanent museum. It even provides rentals. The fifteen spaces of the exhibition, organized by a team led by Caroli, take the garments and objects from this archive.

Both music and fashion have always produced synaesthesia: someone might "see" with their ears and "hear" with their eyes. This exhibition is an affirmation of synaesthetic experience. Fifteen glass showcases contain authentic pieces—clothes, accessories, records, everyday objects—which belong to the history of our century's styles, from American Western to Cyberpunk. In the foggy and trendy atmosphere of Romagna, the show, accompanied by a recorded tape, traces a sensory journey through the jointly evocative media of music ("sound") and clothing ("sight"). The exhibition starts with the American Western style of the 30s and 40s. Blue-jeans were then becoming part of a common dress code rather than simply working clothes. Jackets with fringe, pointed boots and cowboy hats appeared in the halls where people danced (and still dance) to the sounds of country music. Beach Boys' Surfer notes accompany the exhibits in the second showcase. To their music people wore Catalina T-shirts and practised outdoor sports. Then we pass on to a 1950s Rockabillie showcase and Elvis Presley's image, which served as a model for a generation of young people. Following on is the U.K.: Teddy Boys, young proletarians remembered for refined clothes and music; Mods, with their stiff collars, narrow ties and The Who music; Psychedelics, fans of Pink Floyd who tried LSD and sported textiles that we would today call "new materials"; and finally Skinheads, hard-living and anarchic, with their shaven heads, boots and Screwdriver Rock.

Back in the U.S.A., the Hippies-rebels of the 60s from Berkeley to Woodstock are represented through Jimi Hendrix's and Janis Joplin's music, patchwork garments, low-waist bell-bottom jeans, Afghan jackets and string bags. Bob Marley's bristly icon, reggae sounds and Rasta-farian multicolor textiles follow. Next, a sort of quotation: the Skaters are the sports tribe of the 70s, heirs of the Surfers, but their boards are made for the urban concrete and not for Pacific waves.

Then we arrive at the style *par excellence* which has both appropriated and parodied preceding and future styles and fashions: Punk, whose obscene minstrels were the Sex Pistols. Punk was an expression of surrealism in dress and music, a British paradox that made use of every possible body modification, from cutting to piercing to tattooing. In the 80s, Goths veiled themselves and dressed in black velvet while listening to Bauhaus and the Sisters of Mercy. This is juxtaposed with Heavy Metal fans, whose garments and music required rough, cacophonous tones. The 90s' Hippie renaissance is represented by Grunge style, with its unbleached wool garments and check shirts, accompanied by the sound of Nirvana. Finally, the beginning of the future: Cyberpunk projects virtual journeys through music as bodies dive through cables, optical fibres and NASA textiles.

Angelo Caroli says: "Young people come here to look at their roots while their elders relive their memories. They can all verify how much even the more eccentric street styles have influenced fashion and everyday clothing." He is right; in the 70s people wore Hippie styles unself-consciously and designers were inspired by Woodstock snapshots. In the 80s and 90s Versace revived Punk in an absolutely unique way. We can admire Caroli's rigor in the choice of materials from his collection. His collecting began twenty years ago when the "second-hand" market was frequented by a few enthusiasts who would re-use clothes once belonging to ordinary people. The fascination of this vintage archive consists in the value of unique pieces that everyone and anyone can make new through fresh interpretations. Style is more than fashion, because it is made up of emotions, memories, culture and history. This is why the Vintage Palace is a place where these artistic works assume a further value, beyond the reality expressed in the eye of the beholder.

Vintage Palace has organized various other exhibits as well as historical and social events. Many Italian musical production companies come here for their videoclips, and television production companies for their costumes. Angelo Caroli and Mario Gulmanelli possess one of the most important collections of denim clothing in Europe. It was, in fact, used by Levi's Europe for advertising shots. A loving attention informs this exhibition and the whole Vintage Palace collection: the attention of someone who knows that clothing can be profoundly evocative of other times and other places.

Fashion Theory, Volume 3, Issue 1, pp.131–134
Reprints available directly from the Publishers.
Photocopying permitted by licence only.
© 1999 Berg. Printed in the United Kingdom.

**Reviewed by
Anne Massey**

Book Review

Undressing Cinema: Clothing and Identity in the Movies, Stella Bruzzi, (Routledge, 1997)

Undressing Cinema: Clothing and Identity in the Movies offers a significant addition to the fields of both fashion history and film studies. For the first time, the use of clothing in the cinema is isolated and analyzed using methodologies derived from film and cultural studies. As such, it is an illuminating account of dress on film, which ranges freely across the decades of the twentieth century with aplomb. The central themes of race and gender are confidently tackled, as is the key issue of identity.

Stella Bruzzi has produced an important addition to the current body of work on the links between fashion and the screen. This includes the painstaking work of German collectors, Regine and Peter Engelmeier, in their edited collection, *Fashion in Film* (Munich, 1997) or Elizabeth Leeses's *Costume Design and the Movies* (New York, 1991). These books contain important catalogues of key designers' work, exhaustive filmographies and beautiful photographs. What they lack is any engagement with critical theory or cultural analysis. They celebrate the work of the 'hero' designer, but barely acknowledge the role of clothing in narrative or in relation to spectatorship. This is where Bruzzi's work triumphs. It applies recent approaches to narrative, representation and identity, and it is written with fresh, post-feminist conviction.

The book is divided into three main sections, which deal in turn with costume drama, gender and cross-dressing. The contribution of haute-couture designers to the celluloid plot are covered at a dazzling pace in Chapter 1—from Coco Chanel through Hubert de Givenchy to Vivienne Westwood. Bruzzi argues that fashion on the screen may act as a disruption of narrative rather than a reinforcement of it. In her discussion of the costume film, particularly *Picnic at Hanging Rock* (Peter Weir, 1975) and *The Piano* (Jane Campion, 1993), clothing is seen as a symbol of erotic opportunity, as fetishized objects that speak directly to the spectator outside the narrative. The book's coverage of issues around masculinity is dealt with by means of the gangster film, with its preoccupation with flash clothes and expensive accessories. Examples include *Goodfellas* (Martin Scorsese, 1990) and *Reservoir Dogs* (Quentin Tarantino, 1992). There is a fascinating review of the use of clothing in relation to the blaxploitation films of the 1970s and a revisionist treatment of the power of the *femme fatale*. There is also a sensitive analysis of cross-dressing in *Glen or Glenda* (Edward D. Wood Jr. 1954), which however unnecessarily bemoans the film's lack of aesthetic merit.

Whilst the book may, at times, read like an unrelated string of observations about different cinematic moments without a core thesis, this is not unknown in academic work on the cinema. More worrying is the apparently random sprinkling of historical writing without explanation. The consideration of Simone de Beauvoir in relation to the *femme fatale* is understandable; but the book tends to lurch without explanation at times—from a discussion of *Reservoir Dogs*, complete with a quote from Tarantino, to a discussion of early twentieth-century German sociologist and philosopher, Georg Simmel. The first writer to comment on conspicuous consumption, Thorstein Veblen, is mentioned straight after an analysis of *Casino* (Martin Scorsese, 1995), and so on. More recent work on consumption by Daniel Miller or Colin Campbell might have been more appropriate at these points. I also regret the lack of consideration of audience, as opposed to spectatorship. Films considered in *Undressing Cinema*, such as *The Great Gatsby* (Jack

Clayton, 1974) or *Shaft* (Gordon Parks, 1971), made an enormous impact on streetstyle that isn't considered; but perhaps that is not the purpose of the book. Film studies has recently taken on the audience as a legitimate area for consideration, in line with a more empirical approach to the history of cinema and a greater consideration of its context. There could have been more on cinema's influence on fashion on the street, more on its influence on the male T-shirt, more on the film-inspired revival of glamor during the early 1970s. However, the book does succeed in its attempt to theorize an underdeveloped area. But the problem with theory when it's applied in a postmodern *bricolage* sense is that history and depth are sometimes lost.

Fashion Theory, Volume 3, Issue 1, pp.135–138
Reprints available directly from the Publishers.
Photocopying permitted by licence only.
© 1999 Berg. Printed in the United Kingdom.

**Reviewed by
Rebecca Arnold**

Book Review

British Fashion Design, Rag Trade or Image Industry?, Angela McRobbie, (Routledge, 1998)

208 pp., no illustrations, notes, bibliography, index

As a sociologist, Angela McRobbie has sought to employ the methods of her discipline to analyze the working practices of Britain's post-war fashion industry. Drawing largely on the work of Pierre Bourdieu as a theoretical framework, her book discusses the design process, from the art school education of young fashion designers, to their careers in the industry, as well as their relationship to the manufacture and production of garments and the media that is so vital in creating and promoting the imagery that surrounds fashion. At the heart of her study are interviews undertaken with 18 graduates describing their early transition into the world of design, along with discussions with 8 more established designers covering the mid-eighties to mid-nineties. All are London-based (despite forays abroad to work for couturiers), and the younger designers are ex-students of a London art college. These are supplemented with comments from a spectrum of fashion insiders, from college course leaders to journalists and manufacturers.

These interviews provide an interesting and rare insight into the realities of the fashion industry. Most remain anonymous, since their comments cover potentially delicate matters such as course policies and company working practices. This is understandable, but a shame, since more knowledge about the interviewees would have added to the analysis of their ideas about the industry, and their particular perspectives. Also, the focus on London (which McRobbie herself recognizes as a localized, and therefore potentially problematic, aspect of the study), and on graduates from a college that trains in conceptually-based design, gives a particular wash to their comments, and their drive to be viewed as artists who remain true to their own creativity, even if this means an insecure and continually shifting career path. If students from more business—or technology—orientated courses had been included, or those from outside London, this would perhaps have tempered the conclusions that McRobbie draws on the desire of fashion designers to lean towards fine art rather than popular culture. However, her discussion of the problems for fashion in gaining status within the traditional art school system is interesting, illuminating what she calls fashion's "double discourse" of being caught between art and craft, and the seemingly conflicting connotations these words imply.

Her discussion of the work patterns of the graduates reveals the precarious existence of fashion designers. Her interviewees chart a course between the elitist ateliers of European couture houses (which pay poorly, if at all, expecting dedication and good design ideas, despite harsh treatment), and a series of attempts to set up their own labels, the key aspiration of all fashion students, especially those from a conceptual, art school background. Frequently forced into "self-exploitation," working long hours with little pay, and relying on the (since discontinued) government Enterprise Allowance Scheme for top-up money, most accumulated huge debts and several even suffered bankruptcy. For the more established designers the pattern was similar, with even seemingly successful businesses being propped up by necessary freelance work for larger, more commercial companies. McRobbie points to the conscious ignorance of manufacturing and production processes as a major downfall for many such designers and for students trained to value art over craft. She believes that better knowledge of these practicalities would prevent designers being ripped off by Cut Make and Trim firms that frequently farm out work to a series of underpaid, usually female workers, who suffer appalling work conditions, again for little financial reward. The result is a micro-economy of clusters of small scale and home workers, a cottage industry of designers and makers. McRobbie sees greater collaboration between these false polarities, along with more sympathetic government policy, as crucial to improving both conditions and working methods.

Having elaborated on this need for a "new" rag trade, the author moves on to evaluate the role of the fashion media, the image-makers, from PRs to stylists and journalists. She finds an equally fluid and flexible workforce producing images which, she feels, are completely detached from the reality of the garments themselves, or the act of actually selling the designs featured. It is strange that while McRobbie recognizes the importance of images, she denies that they can have depth of meaning, or that they can act as a critique of prevailing ideas and ideals of beauty, gender, status and so on. Her denial of the power of the images to do more than espouse the artistic credentials of their creators perhaps adds to her assertion that there are two quite separate realms of fashion consumption: the actual purchase of garments, and the visual consumption of the image. However, the two spheres are surely linked; designers are so keen to have their work included in magazines because it means that the garments do sell, their cachet as objects enhanced and validated by this process along with that of the designer's status.

McRobbie herself acknowledges that she comes to this project as a sociologist, keen to demystify the workings of the fashion industry rather than to plot its stylistic history, and while this is undoubtedly a welcome endeavor to enrich fashion studies and open up a dialogue between different discourses, it has also raised its own problems. Her interpretation of broadsheet journalists' calling the early nineties grunge trend, "deconstruction," as an example of an attempt to ally fashion with art and intellectualism instead of popular culture, is debatable. Deconstruction was, and remains, a separate form of fashion, with its own evolution quite apart from grunge, even if there was a degree of overlap between the two during grunge's brief reign. Perhaps what the book suggests is that, just as McRobbie calls for greater collaboration between different branches of the fashion industry, there should be a similar bridge-building between fashion studies and sociology, drawing together the methodologies and knowledge from each to add to our overall understanding of this complex and multi-faceted subject.

Fashion Theory, Volume 3, Issue 1, pp.139–140
Reprints available directly from the Publishers.
Photocopying permitted by licence only.
© 1999 Berg. Printed in the United Kingdom.

The Costume Society's Millennium Conference, Royal Armouries Museum, 2–4 July 1999

The Costume Society's Millennium Conference, *Arms and the Man*, will focus on men's wear for protection, identification and warfare and explore how these images have been adapted for fashion and the catwalk. Protective clothing produces its own dress code and its function dictates special textiles and techniques, all of which are reflected in the arts, in design and in society.

Key speakers are in place to present talks on specialists of *Arms and the Man*. A call for papers has been issued and a student's bursary is available.

For further information search the net on:

http://www.bath.uk.com/costumesociety/

or write to:

Judy Tregidden, 25 Church Crescent, Finchley, London N3 1BE.

Fashion Theory, Volume 3, Issue 1, pp.141–142
Reprints available directly from the Publishers.
Photocopying permitted by licence only.

Fins-des-Siècles, The Costume Society and the National Gallery, 6 February and 5 June 1999

As we approach not only the end of this century but also the end of the millennium it is timely to look back at the clothes that our ancestors wore at the end of previous centuries.

These two study days, organized in partnership with the National Gallery, London will explore the clothing and fashions that were worn during the 1790s and 1890s. The Costume Society has gathered together some of the most highly thought of speakers and writers in the field of dress history to give detailed insights into different aspects of clothing at the end of each century.

Each study day will cover one of the decades and speakers will explore the clothing of monarchs and commoners, high fashion and street fashion. They will examine the use of fashion plates and fashion dolls and look at the politics of fashion in the age of the Revolution. Speakers will describe the costumes designed for the popular Gilbert and Sullivan productions of the 1890s and the outrageous creations of the aristocracy for the famous Devonshire House Fancy Dress Ball.

The study day on Saturday, 6 February 1999 will look at Dress in the 1790s and the study day on Saturday, 5 June 1999 will look at Dress in the 1890s. Both will take place at the National Gallery, London. Speakers will include Diana Donald, Aileen Ribeiro, Susan North, John Styles and Philip Warren.

Further information will be available from the National Gallery, Trafalgar Square, London WC2N 5DN. Tickets will be available nearer to the actual study day dates but if you wish to receive booking forms as they become available you may leave your name and address on the recorded message line: 0171 747 2888.

Fashion Theory, Volume 3, Issue 1, pp.143–144
Reprints available directly from the Publishers.
Photocopying permitted by licence only.
© 1999 Berg. Printed in the United Kingdom.

**Courtauld History
of Dress
Association
Conference**

Fashion and Eroticism

**19 and 20 July 1999
Kenneth Clark Lecture Theatre, Courtauld Institute of
Art, Somerset House, Strand, London WC2R 0RN**

This conference will examine the role eroticism plays in the development
of male and female fashions in contemporary and historical contexts.
Papers will consider art historical, literary and mixed media approaches
towards covert and overt eroticism in dress, alongside research undertaken, or in progress, within the field of costume and fashion history.
Speakers will include research students, academics and curators of
relevant collections.

Further information about the programme for the conference can be obtained from the co-ordinator, Valerie Cumming at the following address, or by faxing her on 0171 924 2955.

Valerie Cumming
36A Prince of Wales Drive
London SW11 4SF

Fashion Theory, Volume 3, Issue 1, pp.145–146
Reprints available directly from the Publishers.
Photocopying permitted by licence only.
© 1999 Berg. Printed in the United Kingdom.

Pasold Lecture: 'The Fabric of Fashion'

Wednesday 24 November 1999, 6.00 pm.
Kenneth Clark Lecture Theatre, Courtauld Institute of
Art, Somerset House, Strand, London WC2R 0RN

This is the first lecture in an annual series of public lectures, sponsored by the **Pasold Research Fund**, designed to stimulate interest in all aspects of textile history and is open to all with an interest in this field. The theme of this lecture is the interdependence of art and textiles in the history of fashion. It surveys some of the many materials used to create clothing over the centuries and how they have been represented by artists. Tickets are not needed. Admission free.

The **Pasold Research Fund** supports all aspects of textile history through conferences, small grants, the journal *Textile History*, and a book series, published by Oxford University Press. If you would like to know more, please contact: Dr. Mary B. Rose, Director, Pasold Research Fund, Department of Economics, The Management School, Lancaster University, Lancaster LA1 4YX.

Notes for Contributors

Articles should be approximately 25 pages in length and *must* include a three-sentence biography of the author(s). Interviews should not exceed 15 pages and do not require an author biography. Film, exhibition and book reviews are normally 500 to 1,000 words in length. The Publishers will require a disk as well as a hard copy of any contributions (please mark clearly on the disk what word-processing program has been used).

Fashion Theory: The Journal of Dress, Body & Culture will produce one issue a year devoted to a single topic. Persons wishing to organize a topical issue are invited to submit a proposal which contains a hundred-word description of the topic together with a list of potential contributors and paper subjects. Proposals are accepted only after review by the journal editor and in-house editorial staff at Berg Publishers.

Manuscripts
Manuscripts should be submitted to: *Fashion Theory: The Journal of Dress, Body & Culture*. Manuscripts will be acknowledged by the editor and entered into the review process discussed below. Manuscripts without illustrations will not be returned unless the author provides a self-addressed stamped envelope. Submission of a manuscript to the journal will be taken to imply that it is not being considered elsewhere for publication, and that if accepted for publication, it will not be published elsewhere, in the same form, in any language, without the consent of the editor and publisher. It is a condition of acceptance by the editor of a manuscript for publication that the publishers automatically acquire the copyright of the published article throughout the world. *Fashion Theory: The Journal of Dress, Body & Culture* does not pay authors for their manuscripts nor does it provide retyping, drawing, or mounting of illustrations.

Style
U.S. spelling and mechanicals are to be used. Authors are advised to consult *The Chicago Manual of Style (14th Edition)* as a guideline for style. *Webster's Dictionary* is our arbiter of spelling. We encourage the use of major subheadings and, where appropriate, second-level subheadings. Manuscripts submitted for consideration as an article must contain: a title page with the full title of the article, the author(s) name and address, and a three-sentence biography for each author. Do not place the author's name on any other page of the manuscript.

Manuscript Preparation
Manuscripts must be typed double-spaced (including quotations, notes, and references cited), one side only, with at least one-inch margins on standard paper using a typeface no smaller than 12pts. The original manuscript and a copy of the text on disk *(please ensure it is clearly marked with the word-processing program that has been used) must* be submitted, along with black and white *original* photographs (to be returned). Authors should retain a copy for their records. Any necessary artwork *must* be submitted with the manuscript.

Footnotes

Footnotes appear as 'Notes' at the end of articles. Authors are advised to include footnote material in the text whenever possible. Notes are to be numbered consecutively throughout the paper and are to be typed double-spaced at the end of the text. (Do not use any footnoting or end-noting programs which your software may offer as this text becomes irretrievably lost at the typesetting stage.)

References

The list of references should be limited to, and inclusive of, those publications actually cited in the text. References are to be cited in the body of the text in parentheses with author's last name, the year of original publication, and page number—e.g., (Rouch 1958: 45). Titles and publication information appear as 'References' at the end of the article and should be listed alphabetically by author and chronologically for each author. Names of journals and publications should appear in full. Film and video information appears as 'Filmography'. References cited should be typed double-spaced on a separate page. *References not presented in the style required will be returned to the author for revision.*

Tables

All tabular material should be part of a separately numbered series of 'Tables'. Each table must be typed on a separate sheet and identified by a short descriptive title. Footnotes for tables appear at the bottom of the table. Marginal notations on manuscripts should indicate approximately where tables are to appear.

Figures

All illustrative material (drawings, maps, diagrams, and photographs) should be designated 'Figures'. They must be submitted in a form suitable for publication without redrawing. Drawings should be carefully done with black ink on either hard, white, smooth-surfaced board or good quality tracing paper. Ordinarily, computer-generated drawings are not of publishable quality. Photographs should be black and white glossy prints (the publishers will not accept color) and should be numbered on the back to key with captions. Whenever possible, photographs should be 8 x 10 inches. All figures should be numbered consecutively. All captions should be typed double-spaced on a separate page. Marginal notations on manuscripts should indicate approximately where figures are to appear. While the editors and publishers will use ordinary care in protecting all figures submitted, they cannot assume responsibility for their loss or damage. Authors are discouraged from submitting rare or non-replaceable materials. It is the author's responsibility to secure written copyright clearance on *all* photographs and drawings that are not in the public domain.

Criteria for Evaluation

Fashion Theory: The Journal of Dress, Body & Culture is a refereed journal. Manuscripts will be accepted only after review by both the editors and anonymous reviewers deemed competent to make professional judgments concerning the quality of the manuscript. Upon request, authors will receive reviewers' evaluations.

Reprints for Authors

Twenty-five reprints of authors' articles will be provided to the first named author free of charge. Additional reprints may be purchased upon request.